BEING JOSEPH

―― Being Believers ――

BEING JOSEPH

The Brother Who Restored a Family
and Nurtured a Nation

Rev. Archie Murray

BEING JOSEPH
Copyright © 2018 by Rev. Archie Murray

All rights reserved. Neither this publication nor any part of this publication may be reproduced or transmitted in any form or by any means, electronic or mechanical, including photocopying, recording or any information storage and retrieval system, without permission in writing from the author.

Scripture quotations are taken from the New King James Version®. Copyright © 1982 by Thomas Nelson. Used by permission. All rights reserved.

Printed in Canada

ISBN: 978-1-4866-1573-5

Word Alive Press
119 De Baets Street, Winnipeg, MB R2J 3R9
www.wordalivepress.ca

Cataloguing in Publication may be obtained through Library and Archives Canada

CONTENTS

Introduction ix

SECTION I: BEGINNINGS
1. The Beginning of Things 3
2. Naming Things 5
3. Childhood Things 7
4. Whose History Is This? 13

SECTION II: JOSEPH, BEING SEVENTEEN
5. Joseph, Being Seventeen Years Old 17
6. Ontological Things 19
7. Spiritual Things 23

SECTION III: SEEING OR NOT SEEING
8. Blind to Things 27
9. Reporting Things 29
10. Love Gone Wrong 31

SECTION IV: DREAMS
11. Dreams 37
12. Just a Dream? 41
13. An Experienced Killer 43
14. Entertaining a Thought 47

SECTION V: BEING SENT
15. Injustice! 53
16. Senior Things 55
17. Come and Go 57
18. The Prayer Meeting 59
19. Things of the Spirit 63

SECTION VI: WITHOUT DOUBT

20. Renaming Things — 69
21. Fantasy — 73
22. Reuben — 75
23. Selling Things — 77
24. Sweet Things — 79
25. Where Shall I Go? — 81
26. Without Doubt — 83
27. Judah and Tamar — 87

SECTION VII: EGYPT

28. Egypt in Joseph's Time — 95
29. A Successful Man — 97
30. The Lord Was with Him — 101
31. Joseph, Being Handsome — 103
32. Being Vulnerable — 111

SECTION VIII: BEING IN PRISON

33. Being in Prison — 119
34. Being Angry — 123
35. Being Sad — 127
36. Being Humble — 131
37. Being Restored — 139

SECTION IX: FAMINE

38. Being in Need — 147
39. Being Powerful — 151
40. Being Twelve Brothers — 163
41. Being Guilty — 169
42. Being Honest — 175
43. Pistachio Nuts — 181

44.	Being Astonished	185
45.	Being Confused	191
46.	Joseph Revealed	197

SECTION X: BEING RESTORED

47.	Don't Die Before You're Dead	207
48.	Seeing Visions Again	213
49.	Jacob, Being Settled	217
50.	Being in Goshen	225

SECTION XI: REST

51.	Being Blessed	231
52.	Closing Family Matters	237
53.	Jacob Dying	241
54.	Being Watched…Mourning	245
55.	The Corryvreckan Whirlpool of Doubt	249
56.	Joseph's Reassurance to His Brothers	253
57.	Death of Joseph	255

About the Author	257

INTRODUCTION

This book is written first from a pastoral perspective, then, second, for practical application to the Christian believer's life. We are given the great privilege in the Bible of seeing the mistakes of others. Surely we would be fools to not attempt to learn from them.

The lives of the Old Testament characters are told with almost cruel openness. Their good deeds and bad attitudes, their sins with all their details, and their repentance—instantly or only after years of hardship—are all there. Their private lives are open to us to examine for our good.

In this book we will look at the life of Joseph. He's a beautiful character with very few, if any, faults at all! However, he's surrounded by many people with many faults, all of whom confront him and cause him to suffer. In the Old Testament narrative we are invited, then, to regularly stop reading, take note, meditate, and learn.

The book is intended for all ages and all types of people. We are, after all, simply looking at a life that in great measure was just like our own. We see Joseph infrequently in his childhood and in detail in his teenage years. As he grows into manhood we are privileged to view his rare beauty and the failures of his family and others around him. In it all God is working out His own great plan of salvation. He will bring Jacob and his twelve sons to Egypt to make a nation of slaves into the greatest nation in the world, from which will come the Messiah, the Christ child, Jesus, the Saviour of sinners.

The times and cultures are ancient, around 1650 BC. Yet we are drawn to the characters because they are perfectly recognizable, easy to relate to, and just like us! After all, what is new about favouritism, family strife, hatred, travelling to foreign lands, fortunes rising and falling, relationships, and all the drama therein? These are the substance of daily life in every generation, nation, and culture. The follower of Jesus Christ is able to see in this story how to act in faith as Joseph did. He looked at the world and his circumstances through spiritual eyes and expressed attitudes and reactions that pleased God. Joseph's older brothers, on the other hand, failed in this. They allowed their carnal natures to rule their responses and their hearts.

Hopefully you will think deeper about the Bible characters and stories as we see behind the scenes and cautiously read between the lines. This book is not intended to be theologically heavy; nor is it aimed at typological issues as such. Both of these and many other approaches to the Scriptures are evident in the course of the book, but the focus of the author is to enrich ordinary believers' lives by introducing them to the details of events that are passed over if we read too quickly.

Whoever you may be, whatever you do, you must become aware of who you are, in the deepest sense, in your own heart and mind and self-awareness, and above all you must come to know yourself before God and among men.

The aim of the book is to increase your love for God's Holy Word and to enrich your daily lives in this difficult world today.

SECTION I:
BEGINNINGS

chapter one

THE BEGINNING OF THINGS

Rachel had no children of her own, but she had given children to her husband, Jacob—in a sort of way! They were born to his other wives. So often, the schemes of the natural man look something like a solution. Here they produced children. Yet deep down we sense that this was not what God had in mind to solve Rachel's problem. The children born would be the heads of the tribes of Israel, and God would use them to further His purposes. He would bless them. But they were not Rachel's children!

Of course Rachel knew this because she remained barren. There would be no real fruitfulness, no Joseph, until Rachel touched the throne of God, and He intervened. Rachel did, God did, and Joseph was born. This is such a fundamental subject for our understanding of how God works.

Spiritual children are born of God. Spiritual answers are defined by the intervention of God, in one way or another. *"That which is born of the flesh is flesh, and that which is born of the Spirit is spirit"* (John 3:6). The flesh never crosses over, never morphs into the spirit! The beginning of things is determined by their very being, so spiritual things remain spiritual and worldly things remain worldly. Jesus said we must be *"born again"* (John 3:3). A new life is what He gives—a spiritual life to set against the life of the flesh.

What if Rachel had prayed sooner? It appears that she tried every other human method before she turned to prayer! What if she had prayed first? Would Joseph have arrived sooner? We don't know, but it's doubtful, because God is working to a plan. It's not rigid in its daily outworking, but it determines His overall purposes. He had reasons for keeping Rachel waiting. It may not even have been Rachel He was waiting for! It was His plan that mattered.

Rachel eventually stopped trying to fix things herself. She stopped struggling and it appears from the narrative that she did turn to prayer, because the Bible says that the Lord heard Rachel's cry (Genesis 30:22). This is a change in her. Prayer takes all that striving away, and it brings a humble submissive rest in the Lord, a dovelike peace.

Mary, the mother of Jesus, is such a beautiful example of this spirit. She submissively embraced the call to bear the Christ child. She quietly accepted God's call. Our acceptance of the will of God often requires an enormous spiritual, psychological, cultural, and religious challenge. Mary gave the world a beautiful feminine declaration of this submission. Rachel was perhaps a mere shadow of Mary, but Joseph was born!

How timelessly attractive this humble, submissive spirit is in the Lord's children! It's never slavish. It never reduces the subject. Often, the more genuine the humility and the more deep the submission, the more the individual is exalted! Look at Mary. She had such a beautiful spirit that the greatest civilizations of all time have exercised themselves to declare it, to depict it, to carve it and canvas it, to voluminously fill libraries with it. In their music, art, and literature they extol, in countless languages and nations, this spirit in Mary. Also, and more so, it's seen in the Lord Jesus Christ when He said, *"Not My will, but Yours, be done"* (Luke 22:42).

The Holy Bible, inspired by God, records this submission in ordinary people in their acceptance of His will when faced with the problems of life. We see this in the story of Joseph. His ordinary life was full of problems without an apparent point. His mind must have been full of questions, perhaps like yours. He was, after all, just a youth when our story starts proper, Joseph being seventeen years of age.

chapter two

NAMING THINGS

Joseph would have been told about his own birth. It was such an answer to prayer! It was such an intervention! What mother would not tell her child about that? Rachel would have told him how she had wanted a child and hoped and failed and then rested, and finally he was born, in answer to her prayer. She felt it all so clearly. She wanted to record it so that everyone would understand that her child was a blessing from God. Her spiritual joy at his arrival was expressed by giving him a meaningful name—Joseph!

Would to God that every mother viewed every newborn child with great expectations and also with an infinite anticipation. That is, that each new life would be seen in the light of what an infinite God can do, both in and through it! Oh that conception itself would be restored in our society to such heights of positive awareness and that every birth would be understood to be something to be rejoiced in!

Joseph! His name means "God will add." The practice of expressing our gratitude and joy at childbirth by the use of biblical names or at least meaningful names for our children was common in the Western world until very recently. The name *Joseph* conveys something about God. Rachel experienced God blessing her miraculously. Further, she believed this would not be a single experience. She therefore declared to one and all that "God will add." Rachel encourages us not to limit the Almighty. There's no limit to how often the Lord can bless you—He's not stingy! God will add yet more blessings to you!

When Rachel is rejoicing over Joseph, she's not restricting her thoughts to naming him or to the delivery of her first child. She's not seeing only the full term of the pregnancy as God's hand upon her. Her life of barrenness, her lifetime struggle, her late pregnancy, the birth—these are all seen by her as one continuous and connected event. This is the world view of those who believe that *"He is, and that He is a rewarder of those who diligently seek Him"* (Hebrews 11:6). They see all of life as one continuous dealing with a good God.

Make sure that you publicly acknowledge such blessings in your life. And always be watching in humble submission for His next intervention, His next deliverance, His next providence, in your life.

chapter three

CHILDHOOD THINGS

In this narrative about Jacob and his family we are not told a lot about Joseph in the period from his birth until he was seventeen years of age. However, during his childhood years his family went through some amazing experiences as God dealt with Jacob, his father. This chapter looks at ten or twelve years of Joseph's childhood, to examine briefly the influences on him as a youth. The years from age six to seventeen are formative in our lives. Let's take a brief survey of the events over that period and see how they affected the boy.

Joseph was around six years old when his father, Jacob, left his father-in-law's house to return to Canaan. On this journey Jacob was met by the *"angels of God"* at Mahanaim (Genesis 32:1). Did the six-year-old Joseph hear about this? We don't know for certain, but what a memorable story for a child! God sends His angels to look after His children.

His father got up in the morning one day and limped for the rest of his life! "Dad, why are you limping?" Did Jacob, a father who loved his son, tell him how he had met with God during the night hours (Genesis 32:31) and how he had been affected by that meeting, that his very name had to be changed from *Cheat* to *Prince*, from *Jacob* to *Israel*? This may have been a bit too complicated a story to tell a child, but no doubt it was reinforced many times. God's eternal secret work in the heart is visible to all around—Jacob limped, for the rest of his life! Dads, what a lesson to teach your children—how God has dealt with you in life, at home!

The boy Joseph was present when his father met Esau, his estranged brother (Genesis 33:4). Here Joseph had the opportunity to observe and listen to all the goings-on in the preparation for this meeting. He was at the actual meeting and saw the good parting at the end. These two brothers came from being murderous siblings yet met as long-lost friends and parted as renewed brothers. Surely this will be reflected in the life of Joseph and his siblings in a day to come! He learns the rich benefit of reconciliation, sees forgiveness in action, and feels the warmth of fellowship restored. He may even have observed how his father remained a little uncertain afterwards, despite Esau's warmth.

He was present at Shechem when his father erected an altar called *"El Elohe Israel"* (Genesis 33:20). The boy Joseph may have laid some stones.

Laying stones is something that human beings have done and still do to this day. They feel they have fixed something when they lay a stone. Scottish mountains all have cairns at the top where weary climbers feel the joy and fulfillment of the climb or the walk to the top. They remember these stones all of their lives!

In Joshua 4:21 the people of Israel were told how to answer their children when they saw a stone memorial and asked, *"What do these stones mean?"* Surely Joseph, seeing the altar at Shechem take shape, primitive as it would have been, would have asked about those stones. Did he ask? Someone must have taken time to explain, surely! In Deuteronomy, the Bible counsels God's people to teach God's Word to their children in the real instances of life—*"when you walk by the way"* (Deuteronomy 11:19), *"on the doorposts of your house and on your gates"* (Deuteronomy 11:20), and *"when you sit in your house"* (Deuteronomy 11:19). That's what was happening to Joseph under God's direction.

When a little older and more of a youth than a child, he was present when the "Dinah incidents" occurred (Genesis 34). The incidents themselves from a family perspective are of interest here. Too young to take an active part, would Joseph had heard all the family talk? Would he not even feel in himself, as we might feel as we read, the anger of his brothers? He must have heard the righteous indignation they expressed at their father's objection to their act of retribution. Was he puzzled by their inconsistency? Today, indignant at sin; tomorrow, perhaps not? Joseph learned about the dangers of careless sex—it can result in the death of innocents. Would he not have been surprised, as his brothers were, by his father's lack of response? Would Joseph not, like them, have been openly disappointed in his father? Israel, the prince with God, expressed fear of the surrounding nations (Genesis 34:30–31)! They may have debated timeless questions of the nature of true justice, forgiveness, the right to defend yourself, retribution, crime, and punishment. All these amazing topics may have swirled around his young head. Some of it may have stuck! He saw before he was seventeen that sex is not an innocent play activity.

We can only try to imagine what Joseph learned from these incidents of family life. Children naturally meditate upon events. They are little thinkers! The process is part of the human makeup. God uses these incidents to train us up, to gently shower or to thunder a storm of truth into our young hearts. The inherent force of truth penetrates young hearts and minds even without words, although we are commanded to use words in the training of our children.

In Genesis 35:2–5, Joseph watches as all the adults around him dispose of their foreign idols and the "stuff" of heathen religion. Didn't the boy Joseph experience a revival of true religion in his family at this time? He felt the real and spiritual nature of this act. Surely he sensed a different atmosphere among them as they continued to journey but now exclusively with the God of Abraham, Isaac, and Jacob!

This was a very rare and rich experience for him. It was not simply repairing external relationships in human terms. This was God's people getting right with God! The family got rid of their foreign gods.

Many believers today, and many churches, have never experienced or observed what Joseph saw here as a boy. He learned spiritual resolve. He learned that spiritual repentance is always accompanied with practical expressions. He learned that the process may be tearful, but afterwards it bears forth the peaceable fruits of righteousness. He realized perhaps that God can fill our enemies with fear simply because we have seriously turned to Him.

In Genesis 35:7 Joseph is present on the journey to Bethel and observes his father building an altar there named El Bethel, *"the God of the house of God."* Would not a mother like Rachel take him aside and explain warmly the purpose and meaning of all these things?

Again, in Genesis 35:14, Joseph sees a commemorative stone pillar set up to remind them all, including Joseph, of the event at Bethel. Repetition is a good teacher. God uses it! Joseph again learns that men need to build more than one altar to God in a lifetime. He learns that the altar itself is just a heap of free stones, but every stone represents sacrifice and spiritual depth. Altars are milestones where men meet God in a life-changing way and are changed spiritually. What lessons to learn, and all before you're seventeen!

In Genesis 35:16–20 Joseph is there when his mother dies giving birth to Benjamin. Joseph's name predicted his younger brother Benjamin's birth. What a powerful brotherly connection! Benjamin was that second blessing his mother looked for instantly after Joseph was born. All through Joseph's life Benjamin reminded him that God answers prayer, particularly when you do things God's way! He was a constant reminder of a mother's good testimony.

The whole family is there with his mother Rachel to comfort her both in the birth of Benjamin and in her subsequent dying. Mothers often hold families together. What a loss, the loss of a mother! Joseph learns to deal with grief before he reaches seventeen. But note that the biblical narrative doesn't draw attention to Rachel overmuch. It's Jacob whose history this is, here in the book of Genesis.

In Genesis 35:22, Reuben *"went and lay with Bilhah his father's concubine,"* imagining it was a well-covered secret. But someone told Jacob, his father. Was it Joseph? If it was, he learned the secret that most secrets are not secrets at all!

Genesis 36 gives details about the family of Esau. Joseph is not mentioned in the chapter.

Childhood Things

The Bible is drawing close to the change of narrative that brings Joseph to the fore. The last thing to be mentioned in this preparatory chapter is the death of Isaac (Genesis 35:27–29). At the funeral, would they not recount how Abraham, not so far back in time for them as for us, offered up Isaac, believing that God could, and would, raise him from the dead? Joseph! Are you listening? This is your parentage, your spiritual heritage! You are marked out by God for a purpose...at not yet seventeen!

These are monumental events for one child to have lived through. Surely we will discover lessons and principles he adopted and observe him growing into manhood as we continue to read the history of Jacob.

chapter four

WHOSE HISTORY IS THIS?

This is the history of Jacob. Joseph, being seventeen years old, was feeding the flock with his brothers.
—Genesis 37:2

So, Jacob or Joseph? Here in verse 2 of chapter 37, it looks as though we are moving on in the narrative to look at Joseph. It looks like the history of Jacob has been fully given in the previous chapters, and Joseph is the new subject. Some say that is exactly what is happening in the text.

Jacob will quietly go into the background during the main story of Joseph. However when we later see Jacob go down into Egypt to meet the son he thought was dead and live there for another seventeen years, then it looks very like Jacob just took a back seat while God took control of getting him to Egypt via Joseph. Also not insignificant to this discussion, right now in the story Jacob is not dead! Nor will he be during all of Joseph's difficult and bountiful years. Jacob's history will continue through all these chapters until he does die, but for now it will be told mainly as it relates to his son Joseph.

The story of Joseph is necessary to explain to future generations how Israel the man got to Egypt and how the family of Israel grew to be a nation of slaves in Egypt. So while this part of Genesis now focuses on Joseph, it's still the history of Jacob.

From chapters 30 to 36, everything that happened to Jacob tells us about what was happening to Joseph. Though he's not really mentioned, we know he was there. Then in chapters 37 to 51 the history of Jacob continues as we consider his son Joseph.

Being Joseph

"Jacob dwelt in the land where his father was a stranger, in the land of Canaan" (Genesis 37:1). The Bible gives one last sentence to summarize Jacob before it moves on to Joseph proper. Jacob dwelt in the land where his father was a stranger. The fact that his father was a stranger in this land surely casts colour on the experience of Jacob himself. Otherwise we might ask what the purpose of the comment was. These few words indicate a lack of permanence, a lonely lack of belonging—Jacob had no "home"; Jacob was secretly lost! However, the next sentence is pregnant with purpose and energy: *"Joseph, being seventeen years old"* (Genesis 37:2).

SECTION II:
JOSEPH, BEING SEVENTEEN

chapter five

JOSEPH, BEING SEVENTEEN YEARS OLD

Joseph, being seventeen years old.

—Genesis 37:2

The Bible seems to want us to know that Joseph is seventeen. The entire story pivots on this verse. The previous chapters are bringing us to Joseph being seventeen. The actual story of Joseph begins seriously with the notice that Joseph is seventeen. Perhaps God wants us, as we read, to think about being seventeen years old for a moment. Maybe He wants us to stop and listen and look deeper, and—who knows? We may learn something useful!

There's nothing essentially special about this age. It's not mystically unique in the Scriptures. There's no spiritual "moment" at seventeen. It's just an anonymous age. It's not a landmark age, like twelve or eighteen or twenty, thirty, or forty. Even seventy years of age is given more significance than seventeen! It's just around the middle of teenage years. Yet God takes Joseph and thrusts him into His service at seventeen! So why seventeen years of age? Perhaps for the very reason that it's not a significant age!

Perhaps the insignificance of seventeen is its actual significance here. Perhaps that is why God chose Joseph at seventeen.

Paul says,

> *For you see your calling, brethren, that not many wise according to the flesh, not many mighty, not many noble, are*

called. But God has chosen...the things which are not, to bring to nothing the things that are.
—1 Corinthians 1:26–28

This is a spiritual principle. Joseph's non-special age tells us that there's no special age; in fact, we don't have to be special or significant in any way at all before we can serve God.

We just need to follow Him wherever He takes us.

God took Joseph at seventeen and prepared him for a life of service. Joseph didn't think he was special; his brothers certainly didn't think he was special. Jacob thought Joseph was special all the time, but at that moment when God showed Jacob that his son Joseph *was* special, when Joseph recounted his dream, Jacob rejected it out of hand! Only after he was cautioned by the dream did he begin to realize that God had possibly put His hand upon Joseph and enlisted him into divine service.

To Joseph, "God's hand" looked strangely like his brothers'!

chapter six

ONTOLOGICAL THINGS

Great word to start a chapter with! *Ontological* means "being," existing at its deepest level. It indicates the real person's being. It's a special word. In Hebrew, the "verb..

> [to be] indicates more than simple existence or identity... Rather, the verb makes a strong statement about the being or presence of a person or thing...The verb can be used to emphasize the presence of a person...or a state of being...In such cases, the verb indicates that their presence (or absence) is noticeable—it makes a real difference to what is happening.[1]

In *"Joseph, being seventeen years old"* (Genesis 37:2), the verb seems to emphasize Joseph's essential connection to the event happening when he was seventeen. That for us is the event God is working out in the history of Jacob. For us it might suffice to say that Joseph was important at seventeen years of age or that he was the person he should have been at seventeen years of age.

And we might say that the fact God used him indicates that this was the case with Joseph; he was what he should be, not in any mere moral or physical sense but only in the spiritual sense of the words.

Could there be more opposite statements about two people than *"Jacob dwelt in the land where his father was a stranger"*

---

[1] W. E. Vine, Merrill F. Unger, and William White Jr., *Vine's Complete Expository Dictionary of Old and New Testament Words* (Nashville: Thomas Nelson Publishers, 1985), 13.

(Genesis 37:1) and *"Joseph, being seventeen years old"* (Genesis 37:2)? This state of being tends to suggest that it existed before and after the specific event. Its mention here is to focus our attention on Joseph as being what God wanted him to be at seventeen years of age.

Used of the Lord Jesus Christ in Philippians 2:6, *"who, being in the form of God,"* "the phrase 'who being (huparchon) in the form of God,' implies His preexistent Deity, previous to His birth, and His continued Deity afterwards."[2] The phrase in Genesis 37:2 *"Joseph, being seventeen years old"* is similar. They both state there was something significant about the use of "being" in these Scriptures.

God is certainly telling us not merely Joseph's age as a number but the deeper understanding of what being seventeen was for Joseph. However we are being introduced to something more personal in this text, if we are willing to stop and listen. The reader is being invited by the Bible to stop and ask "What kind of being am I?"

In none of this discussion are we really interested in being seventeen as such. You might be seventeen or any other age, even far removed from seventeen; still, at your own age you are "being"; you are someone! Joseph's being seventeen is merely the catalyst to cause us to consider our whole life, past and present, against the backdrop of our present age. This is our meditation on this verse.

Are you the person you should be at this point in your life? Mark it as an age if you want. But the challenge for us is this: is the being I am right now the being God intended me to be right now? Or has He more to do in me to get me to the place Joseph was at? Then again, it may be that you were like Joseph when you were seventeen, but at a much later age you left that being, and now you are in the shadows, merely existing when you should be being someone special, a child of God.

It may be helpful here to draw a timeline of your own life for yourself. If you are younger than seventeen, draw a line from your present age to age seventeen and map out where your present lifestyle,

---

2   W. E. Vine, *Vine's Expository Dictionary of New Testament Words* (n.p.: Barbour, n.d.), 116.

Ontological Things

habits, attitudes, spiritual practices, Christian life, and disciplines will take you to when you extend the line to seventeen. For example, if you read your Bible carelessly now, you probably will not read it at all by the time you reach seventeen. If you read it diligently now, by seventeen you might be an expert on it, both in personal experience and in general knowledge.

If you are older than seventeen, a timeline of spiritual experience since you were seventeen until the present might show times of sad decline. Maybe it would reveal a slow but significant trend of worldliness, a drop in standards, a change of stance on issues, a lessening of commitment to God's Word, a lazy, unconcerned attitude towards personal holiness, and a carelessness towards your neighbour. You would certainly be challenged and may well find a need to return to things from spiritually better days in time gone by since you were seventeen years old. Perhaps you might be able to correlate your spiritual highs with your daily lifestyle, or perhaps like Joseph you might find no correlation between personal godliness and daily blessings.

Joseph had a mixed bag of what we would call "blessings" in these years after seventeen. All the good was tarnished because he was in a foreign country, away from those he loved. Yet he clearly was in touch with God.

If you are already seventeen, then take courage from Joseph. Age itself is never a condition of service. God will take you as you are, whether you are seventeen or seventy years of age. God had been working in and around Joseph since he was born. Joseph knew much more than he realized. He had been in God's school for seventeen years, the school of God's Daily Life Academy!

We can easily identify some aspects of Joseph's character. The main one, perhaps, is a good close relationship with his father. So start your timeline today and mark out how you will attain a good relationship with your heavenly Father. Pray every day, read the Scriptures, and seriously seek God with all your heart, soul, mind, and strength. Don't be discouraged if you see little progress. Your progress is to be seen by the Lord; you just do the work of walking with the Lord daily and diligently.

There's no essential need for programs or methods, of course. God is available. Talk to Him and listen as He answers you from His Word, the Bible. The best way to affect your being is to spend time—patient, real, truthful, and spiritual time—with God in prayer and meditation on His Word. John Calvin summed up all true knowledge as "knowledge of God and knowledge of self."[3] This is the depth of work that reaches our being. Joseph had been there, perhaps as he meditated on family events down the years.

Sadly for many of us today any examination that goes deep enough to be meaningful—but not deep enough to kill our spirit—would show us as having been reduced to a shadow of the men and women of God we were when we were seventeen years old. When we were seventeen years old, like Joseph, nobody was taking us seriously—except God. Now, perhaps, everyone takes us seriously—except God! Sometimes we need to go back down memory lane, back to the old paths, back to that crossroad or to where we lost the blessing—or found it—by taking the road to the foot of the cross.

---

3   John Calvin, *Institutes of the Christian Religion* (London, England: James Clark and Co., 1962), 37.

chapter seven

SPIRITUAL THINGS

Joseph was seventeen years old when God took him into His service in the most humble of ways. He was sent, but he was to go and be rejected by those to whom he was sent. He would suffer and be abused, cheated, ignored, imprisoned, reviled, exalted, and eventually vindicated.

He was seventeen! About to be taken from familiar things into a whole new world. His childhood was over, and his innocent teenage years were about to close. He was about to be engaged as a man of God.

This move from spiritual childhood to spiritual adulthood can be sudden, even abrupt. God thrusts His servants into service; He doesn't nurse them into service. He "calls" them by name, and they say *"Here am I! Send me"* (Isaiah 6:8). Then they go.

In responding to that call they grow up quickly in mind, lay aside childish things, and become men and women of God. Indeed, they lay aside their lives, take up the cross, and follow Jesus wherever He takes them. They are servants, not masters; they do as they are told, not what they want. They never retire! They are called of God.

Mathew Henry sums up the cost of discipleship and the willing way it's expressed. Of the disciples after the greatest catch they ever had (Luke 5), he says, "It is observable that they *left all to follow Christ*, when their calling prospered in their hands more than ever it had done and they had had uncommon success in it."[4] Most of them died serving. They died like their Master, having earned no signifi-

---

4 Matthew Henry, *Matthew Henry's Commentary on the Whole Bible*, vol. 5, *Matthew to John* (n.p.: Hendrickson Publishers, 1991), 511.

cant wealth in the process of serving. Their sufferings and sacrifices for the gospel are what we read of. Their success is measured in eternal values. The church lives because they died to self.

Many of us are only willing to serve in pleasant, significant, or successful ways. And we assess success and significance by the world's values! We are not rushing to give anything up for Christ! We are more likely to rent out the gifts freely given to us to the first paying customer.

Financial success is never, never, an "essential" sign of a call or a gift given by God. More often the church in history recognized the loss of this world's goods to be evidence of God's hand upon a life. They learned these principles by looking at the lives of God's servants in the Bible, as in the life of Joseph.

Service for God doesn't sanctify or legitimize begging for "support" from God's people. The idea that God's work will never lack God's supply is a statement of faith. God's servants are never beggars! They are God's servants, and He said the workman *"is worthy of his wages"* (1 Timothy 5:18). There are many today claiming to serve God, but He didn't hire them. Don't make God look like He has no money or is stingy. If you have no faith, begging will only expose that!

Spiritual terminology alone doesn't make anything spiritual. God's servants are to take up the cross, to be rejected by the world, to even suffer at the hands of their church family—to suffer for righteousness' sake (Matthew 5:10; 1 Peter 3:14). We are to be convinced that our reward is in heaven, not here in this sad world.

Joseph's experience looks nothing like what we describe today as God's service. What caused us to lose these principles? They were held so clearly and expressed so consistently in the literature of the historic church. Joseph was to be an alien in a strange land, a foreigner, a pilgrim. Those are the descriptive words of both the Old Testament and the New Testament. They are used to describe the child of God, then, and now.

SECTION III: SEEING OR NOT SEEING

chapter eight

BLIND TO THINGS

Joseph, being seventeen years old, was feeding the flock with his brothers.

—Genesis 37:2

The Bible shows us that God's answers are frequently standing right beside us. We engage with them in whatever form they come, but we seldom consider for a moment that they might be what they are. They are our deliverance, our answers to prayer. God's help is seldom far away. We are so slow to understand, so lacking in faith, then and now.

Joseph's brothers were having conversations with Joseph every day; did they hear anything? Perhaps not! This is a constant theme in this story. Be watchful; you may be missing many interventions of God in your life! Be open, looking always for His helping hand.

There was Joseph, God's answer to his brothers' needs, right beside them. They knew his name, but they didn't know him! Day after day he was with them. He talked to them individually, in twos and threes, as a group, but they didn't know who he was. They thought they certainly did know him. They were sure they understood him, to the depth even of the motivation for his actions. They could read his mind and his heart; they understood him to the core of his being. Or so they thought!

Yet they didn't know him or understand him at all. They didn't realize their loss when they sold him. They felt enriched, free! But only for a moment. When life fell apart they didn't connect it with their loss of Joseph. They blamed him who would redeem them!

How like us! How blind and stubborn and how *"slow of heart to believe in all that the prophets have spoken"* (Luke 24:25), as Jesus said of two of His followers. Why were they like this? Joseph stood beside them, and when they looked at him they saw someone entirely different from the Joseph we see when we read the story. This was because God blinded them for His own reasons, to further His own great plan. God did it, but their prejudice gladly embraced blindness, and they refused to see. They thought they had a reasonable case for dismissing him and felt comfortable about killing him.

chapter nine
REPORTING THINGS

And the lad was with the sons of Bilhah and the sons of Zilpah, his father's wives.

—Genesis 37:2

Here the Scripture gently introduces us to one fundamental cause of the problems among these brothers. Joseph's mother, Rachel, had died giving birth to his younger brother, Benjamin. Jacob had four wives, all with different personalities and characters. He had four different sets of children with varied characters and personalities and vulnerabilities to conflict for any number of reasons. Conflicts like we see in Jacob's family are well documented throughout the history of polygamy. Communities that still continue the practice are corrupted by the same injustices. These are the reasons polygamy is rightly outlawed in most Western countries. The family is divided by different mothers. It's conquered before it gets going!

"Joseph brought a bad report of them to his father" (Genesis 37:2). This is not to be seen as a negative comment about Joseph in any way. Some perhaps attribute their own childhood "telltale" attitudes to Joseph, but the Bible doesn't give us grounds to criticize him. On the contrary, the life of Joseph is presented in the Word of God as exemplary.

That the bad report was an accurate report can be seen from the rest of the story. We are not given details as to the content of the report, or reports, that Joseph brought. However, we can assume that God's Holy Word is only keeping us from what would defile us. There will be plenty of evidence of bad behaviour as this story unfolds. Indeed, the Scriptures give a "bad report" about Joseph's brethren!

Prayer

Prayer is, at times, a form of reporting to our heavenly Father about the behaviour of others. We tell the Lord what is seemingly wrong in a situation and ask Him to help those involved. Prayer, if exercised properly, cleanses and balances our thoughts.

When talking among ourselves about other people's sin, we often exaggerate and provoke each other into saying things we perhaps should not have said. However, real prayer tones down the sharpness of the report. God's presence brings us all to the common ground of those who have *"all turned aside"* (Romans 3:12). *"There is none righteous, no, not one"* (Romans 3:10). This should be the cautionary note sounding in our conscience as we pray for the brother who has fallen.

Joseph brought a bad report to his father. A bad report, but a true report. Often, we don't like bad reports because we are more concerned with comfortable feelings than with truth in its essence. "Speak to us of pleasant things." In this Joseph reminds us that conversation about the failures of others should be restricted to talking to God, avoiding the error of gossip, which is more virile than truth. Gossip is like a dust cloud that blinds people to truth. Truth is like the rock after the dust settles that has always been there, unmoved, still exactly as it was, still solidly reliable, like the Word of God itself.

chapter ten

LOVE GONE WRONG

Now Israel loved Joseph more than all his children.
—Genesis 37:3

The first half of this sentence—is it not fatherhood summed up? Is it not complete? Israel loved Joseph!

We are interested in a father's love here. Though it's the most natural thing in the world, it's still timelessly attractive. In this text, the Bible tells us with profound simplicity, so that we should not miss it, *"Now Israel loved Joseph."* Here is a deep comfort for Joseph, a lasting strength, a solid foundation; indeed a total lifelong bond is expressed here.

Surely a hint about the trinity is contained here, and in particular the relationship between God the Father and God the Son. *"This is My beloved Son, in whom I am well pleased"* (Matthew 3:17).

In this recent era particularly, many of us, young and old, wish we had experienced this—to have a father who loved us—but it was denied to us, taken from us, never given. For reasons unknown, we never knew this love. We envy Joseph as we read. What must it have been like?

Then know this: you have a Father who loves you! He knows you by name. He is God the Father, our Father who is in heaven. He is the God and Father of our Lord Jesus Christ. He is the God who so loved the world that He gave His only Son—for you. Never forget this love. Get to know Him through Jesus. He never fails and certainly never leaves. His love is eternal.

If you are a failed father, fix it today. Go home! Start again! Do it right! If this is not possible, live by God's grace as though you were such a father. Do this in a quiet, determined way. Then all who know you will see true fatherhood, now, repentantly fixed in your character.

The second part of the text says, "more than all his children." Jacob loved Joseph more than all his children. Ah! How we human beings manage to take what is perfect and taint it! In saying this the Bible is not excusing or condemning Jacob. It's merely telling us the way things were. Blame is not always a helpful concept.

Jacob made mistakes, public and open. The coat of many colours declared that Joseph was special, for all to see. Of course only the brothers may have noticed! The Scriptures show plainly that Jacob created a difference between the brothers by treating Joseph as special. The Bible doesn't say this is right; it merely gives us an explanation for some of the division that appear as the story unfolds.

It was *"because he was the son of his old age"* (Genesis 37:3). We may see this as a cautious excusing clause. It could be that the Lord is making some space for Jacob in the matter. It should slow us in our rush to judge before taking time to examining ourselves first in the area of our parenting skills. And note that Jacob is being exposed here as an old man.

The Bible doesn't sound like it's condemning Jacob when it says he loved Joseph more than all his children. It's an explanatory note. We are too quick, like the brothers, to rush to blame. The Bible doesn't encourage us to judge, but it does allow us to see the picture in order that we might learn not to be like Jacob in his weakness as a father. Who are we in this age of family disintegration to imagine that we can judge anyone's parenting?

Many good men do go astray in their old age. Never let your guard down when you think you have settled into the life of a believer. When the temptations of youth are past and some of the "old masters" have weakened, sin is still as virile as ever. Sadly, then Satan often sees his opportunity enlarged by our passivity.

By the time Joseph was seventeen, Jacob had become tired and not the man he was in his younger days. He was still the cheat on

Love Gone Wrong

the one hand and the prince on the other. Just like us! How well Paul says it for us in Romans: "*O wretched man that I am!*" (Romans 7:24). So let us, as we read, give Jacob some space and acknowledge that his love may have gone wrong but its basis was very excusable in human terms, very understandable in light of Jacob's special love for Rachel, her long wait for a child, and Joseph's actual arrival.

> *But when his brothers saw that their father loved him more than all his brothers, they hated him and could not speak peaceably to him.*
> —Genesis 37:4

Hate is so powerful an emotion as to lead to murder! Do not treat it lightly! How will you know if this dreadful infection has begun to infiltrate you? You will be unable to *"speak peaceably."* This is the sign the Bible gives of the early presence of hatred in this story. Sadly, this hating didn't go away. Its effect upon the brothers lasted for the entire story, as we shall see.

SECTION IV:
DREAMS

chapter eleven

DREAMS

Now Joseph had a dream, and he told it to his brothers; and they hated him even more.

—Genesis 37:5

This is the issue that raises the problem for these jealous brothers. Joseph wants to tell his brothers about his dream. He approaches them without thought as to how they will respond. He may not understand it, due to his age, but he's seeking a mutual meeting of like minds. But their minds are not "like minds." Joseph is young, too young to really understand, it seems.

They are all older; they should be able to assess matters fairly and reasonably. But we know that their natural ability to relate to people is all upset because of their obsessive hatred. They are not able to accept this young brother, or his dream, no matter how he presents it, no matter how innocent he is. Hatred is quietly, but not peacefully, waiting for such a fuse as this to spark words, sharp words, like shrapnel. Words that cut.

Hatred makes us unable to give others a fair hearing. Hatred distorts our hearing in the first place. Our speech merely follows the road hatred has cut out. Like water being drawn by gravity down through the land, it always finally reaches the lowest point. Before we rationalize or speak, hatred has done its work. It has dug a deep grave for the innocent. It has already buried the speaker. We are beaten before we begin to speak. Hatred corrupts the ability to think or speak fairly. Hatred instinctively knows that a fair hearing will only condemn itself! Often the person speaking knows that their words are distorted, but they can't help themselves.

"So he said to them, 'Please hear this dream which I have dreamed'" (Genesis 37:6). Note Joseph's thoughtful, mannerly approach to the subject of his dream: *"Please hear."* Some accuse Joseph of being an annoying little brother, knowingly provoking the older group. They even accuse him of deliberately provoking them, knowing that he's the favourite son. It's difficult to insert this motive in a life that is otherwise exemplary. Arrogance, especially youthful arrogance, needs no permission to speak. *"Please"* is not in its vocabulary. Joseph says, *"Please hear this dream."*

Throughout Joseph's life, he was the one being targeted for abuse. There was no other occasion where such an attitude was evident in him. These two words *"Please hear"* are much more likely to have been said in an appealing and thoughtful manner than designed to irritate. Further, even if there was an element of provocation, it was surely a simple, even innocent, boyishness, and the older should have known better than the younger!

Nothing is contained in Joseph's words that minimizes the hatred they express. This part of the story shows Joseph as entirely innocent and the brothers as entirely guilty. Joseph is, here again, a picture of Jesus, who also came to His own innocently, yet the Pharisees continually tried to catch Him out in His words. However, the brothers listened with both ears—both distorted!

> *"There we were, binding sheaves in the field. Then behold, my sheaf arose and also stood upright; and indeed your sheaves stood all around and bowed down to my sheaf."*
> —Genesis 37:7

He's telling them about a dream he had, probably the night before. Isn't it possible that he was somewhat confused by the dream? He says, *"Then behold."* The word *behold* is a surprised call to attention, to thoughtful concentration, a request for consideration regarding something that is surprising or unusual.

Dreams

It's quite likely that Joseph has not even begun to think about the meaning of the dream! He doesn't propose possible interpretations, let alone implications. But the dream is unusual, and he considers it worthy of sharing, maybe even to assess its meaning. Joseph, in his innocence, may not even have discerned the obvious statement the dream is making. Like a boat careering towards a waterfall and out of control, moved by a force greater than itself, the brothers rush to interpret the dream.

This is not the time to rush into hasty words! This is a moment to speak very carefully. Dreams are not concrete realities. Dreams don't belong to the realm of legal statements. They are not even rational thoughts. Dreams are hazy, not mystical, as in having hidden meanings. They are not even mythical—that is, totally fantastical and unreal—fantasies. Most dreams are simply mixed up disconnected thoughts, held together by complete nonsense! Nevertheless, we should stop and think when a dream comes out of the night. Whether it lands like a butterfly or hits us like a hurricane, if it stays with us till morning we should reflect on it for at least a brief moment. It's the same for those who listen to a dream. They must give it a different level of listening or it will merely mist away.

Dreams, if held at all, must be held lightly. They are like a vapour. If you aren't careful, you will lose them. You will stir them all up, and they will quickly swirl into nothingness and be lost, even if it is actually no real loss at all!

Joseph is handling his dream wisely. He asks for a quiet reflection, a cautious meditation, a moment of discovery. Not too serious, but serious enough to think about for a moment—that's all! Just in case. Who knows? It might just have significance!

Most of the time a dream should be dismissed as no more than the whimsical thing it was; it was just a dream in the night. Only when the dream remains in the present—that is, it stays with us—is there any chance of it ministering to us.

Dreams, ethereal as they are, need to be listened to rationally and given a little consideration. They may only teach us to eat less late at night. They may only teach us that our stress level is getting out of control. Usually they will be no more than a mere dream, but they may on rare occasions be much more. As in this situation, if only we would be thoughtful, more careful! God, give us the patience to at least listen to our enemy; he may turn out to be our friend!

chapter twelve

JUST A DREAM?

And his brothers said to him.

—Genesis 37:8

Joseph's brothers have no time. They have no sensitivity. Like a disturbed sleeper they lash out, startled, then jump out of bed, throwing covers, and pace to purge the bad dream. They have all, together, instantly, by their rage, named it a nightmare! They also in an instant are filled with a renewed sense of hatred. It's just a dream—isn't it?

Joseph's dream had a certain simplicity. The interpretation is so clear and pure that it can even cut through hatred and be heard with a singular clarity. The brothers would have fit well into that very physical mob when it cried out with an nightmarish harmony, *"Crucify Him, crucify Him!"* (Luke 23:21). As the temple curtain was torn in two (Matthew 27:51), so truth splices hatred and gives access to itself, even to those who oppose it. Joseph's dream spoke for itself; it needed no interpretation. It did, however, require a response!

And his brothers said to him, "Shall you indeed reign over us? Or shall you indeed have dominion over us?" So they hated him even more for his dreams and for his words.

—Genesis 37:8

How right they were in their understanding! How wrong they were in their response! Yet simple and clear as the meaning was, it's still likely that Joseph had no such thoughts then, and perhaps not even until many years later.

Truth always extracts a response. Responses expose us. Even when truth comes in the flimsiest of forms—here in a dream—it exposes the hearts of men. Rejection of truth is never neutral. The act produces an equal and opposite reaction: *"So they hated him even more."*

Read your own heart regularly and see if there is any wicked way in you. Or be brave, like the psalmist who invited the Lord to *"Try me…and see if there is any wicked way in me"* (Psalm 139:23–24).

"Then he dreamed still another dream and told it to his brothers" (Genesis 37:9). If we still need evidence of Joseph's innocence or naivety, surely this is it! He's surely still not seeing things the way his brothers do. Truth does not go away easily.

chapter thirteen

AN EXPERIENCED KILLER

"Look, I have dreamed another dream. And this time, the sun, the moon, and the eleven stars bowed down to me."
—Genesis 37:9

The language seems to suggest a stronger approach, maybe even more confident, more insistent, He says, *"Look,"* meaning, "think about this reasonably." Joseph is still not realizing the extent of his alienation from his brothers. He seems to want a fair family hearing of these dreams and a combined discussion and discovery of what they potentially mean. There will be none of that. He may even want to understand their implications so as to address them. We don't know, but the idea that this is just an irritating little-brother moment is not fair to the language used in the narrative. This is an innocent younger brother.

> *So he told it to his father and his brothers; and his father rebuked him and said to him, "What is this dream that you have dreamed? Shall your mother and I and your brothers indeed come to bow down to the earth before you?"*
> —Genesis 37:10

Jacob says, *"Shall your mother and I...bow down...before you?"* And despite the fact that it's a question of principal (Rachel is dead at this point in time), the reader feels as though someone needs to shout out really loudly, "Yes, that is what he dreamed!" It's a moment when the obvious is clearly understood—there's only one way to read this dream. But we can't accept it. We are incapable of accepting it. We can't even begin to consider it. It cannot be! The story should stop here. There's no more to be said. It's ridiculous. It's unimaginable, even impossible, irrational. It's totally wrong! We feel insulted at the thought of having a discussion on such apparent nonsense. That's the end of that! Move on.

And that's what actually happens. It's as if the conversation never took place. Yet God is the one who wants them to listen! Joseph is just a boy messenger. And the patriarchal norms of their understanding are not allowed to be examined. A radical thought (the dream) is dismissed without discussion. Joseph is roundly outvoted, and silence ensues. Nobody learns; no one is challenged to think or act. No new concepts are born; the old is ratified by a monitored silence.

This is the same family whose progeny would stone the prophets and kill those who are sent to them. This is the spirit that gave birth to those who in a later day would contort and twist inside at the message of Jeremiah and Ezekiel. These are the parents of those whose children to come would kill the Messiah. Yet this spirit, the spirit that refuses to hear, that will not listen to learn, is present in every culture and every realm. It's not a demonic spirit, but it's most definitely a possession! It was taught to mankind by God's own children who first stopped listening to His sweet voice calling in the garden of Eden and brought expulsion to us all. It's still expelling God's servants and God's people who, like Joseph, tenderly appeal for them to "Please hear." It's indeed the normal reaction to challenges to cultural norms in every society. Most upsetting, it's the normal spirit in the church through the ages, with some exceptions. Yet the gospel we believe explodes cultural norms!

The way to defuse challenges to the norms of the church and society is to refuse to speak. Silence is an experienced killer!

Any person or society that deals wisely with legitimate challenges to its concepts will grow and develop in a healthy way, often holding more firmly to what it believed in the first place. Never be afraid of challenges to your position on anything. The challenge—this startling idea—if it is sound will not go away. The thought that

An Experienced Killer

Jacob will bow before his youngest son, or any other thought that puts our focus on our prejudices, will persist. Our critics can be our best aid to improvement if we can be strong enough to listen properly.

Those who resist and reject without consideration have welcomed a host into their hearts. They have cleaned out demons but left the door open for them to bring their friends and start again.

Joseph is not to be seen like his brothers. He stops and resets his thinking by holding the apparent problem—the words, the concept, the challenge—in his mind. He will give them time to mature—a long time, years.

chapter fourteen
ENTERTAINING A THOUGHT

And his brothers envied him, but his father kept the matter in mind.

A long time after Jacob and Joseph, around 384 BC, according to many but without actual evidence, Aristotle said something to the effect that it's the mark of an educated mind to be able to entertain a contrary thought without accepting it or rejecting it instantly. Yet the inability to do this is what we see in the majority of men from ancient times until the present—none more intransigent, more stubborn, than those in the present day!

Jacob gives the same instant interpretation of Joseph's dreams as the brothers did. There's only one way to see these dreams, as far as Jacob is concerned. They mean that Joseph will reign over them all—outrageous! However Jacob's response seems to shows that truth is hitting home. Jacob expresses his objection, even indignation. His position has more weight than the brothers; after all, he's the patriarch of the family! But, unlike the brothers, after he has expressed his instant rejection and insulted feelings, he seems to sense something that needs to be held gently and allowed to develop, something that needs to be given time, that must be protected! We would never have predicted or expected this response. The dream stopped Jacob, and the dream intends to teach the reader this: When about to "bluster," stop and take time to think!

After his outburst, his reaction softens inexplicably, and as the verse tells us, he *"kept the matter in mind."* Is there not a tiny sense of a perceptible peace in this response? A conceptual holding, a cautious anticipation. He doesn't *know*; he has nothing tangible, nothing solid; but there's a tiny, embryonic hope in this ever-so-brief quiet moment. A dream—such an innocent, harmless thing, just like Joseph is. Yet the dream and Joseph will change the whole course of their world, and ours, but this can't be revealed in such an angry, jarring environment. It must be kept in a safe place. Jacob's mind is open to the God of Israel. This is a safe place, so different from the abortive destruction in the minds of the brothers.

This statement captures a moment of depth in him. Jacob can't imagine a set of circumstances that could possibly bring the dream to reality. But he's a man whose senses are attuned to God, a man who through many surprising dealings has seen God do the unexpected, the unpredicted, even close to the ridiculous—indeed, the impossible! So everything in him responds to opportunities for God to intervene. He is hereby cautioned from writing Joseph's dream off, even if it materializes in him bowing before his son. Now that is a real cultural conundrum! Wouldn't Aristotle credit Jacob with being "educated"?

He's left only with a question mark, not even a formulated question. Yet it will stay in his mind for a long time, waiting. It will be given an answer. He will not forget. He will give up! But above all, he will wait.

The question will remain sensible to him but unanswered. It doesn't annoy or irritate. It doesn't keep him awake at nights. But it intrigues. Joseph's innocent dream has been tarnished, like the atmosphere at the table after family tension. Yet, though the signpost is vandalized, the road itself still draws us on to good things to come. At least it says, "This journey isn't finished yet." When? How? What? He doesn't know, but the suspended question is the evidence that there will be an answer. It tells Jacob that God is going to do something, maybe! And that's enough for the old man of God to sit with, for now. So he *"kept the matter in mind."*

"And his brothers envied him" (Genesis 37:11). The Bible tells us that the brothers envied Joseph. Why did they envy him? Was it

because they saw something in their father as he listened and responded to Joseph's dream? Jacob, after his initial response, said nothing else. But perhaps a look on his face, a tilt in his posture, a hand on his chin, or his head bent in thoughtfulness alerted them. We don't know, but verse 11 puts both responses in the same sentence: *"And his brothers envied him, but his father kept the matter in mind."*

Body language isn't new. Adam and Eve adopted a posture of fear, hiding among the trees of the garden. The brothers adopted a posture of rebellion, hiding among angry words. But they read their father well and found in him a peaceful acceptance of Joseph's dream. This is a beautiful, thoughtful father-son moment.

Is their envy an improvement? Perhaps it is, in the sense that they let the matter go. It's not spoken of again for a while in the narrative. It hasn't left their minds altogether. They are not changed in their hatred. But the issue seems to have been subdued and left to smoulder.

When a dream given by God is held like Jacob holds it, it becomes a solid, silent anchor in the storms of life. Jacob will need such an anchor quite soon as he faces the apparent death of his son. On one hand, there will be no body to provide absolute closure. On the other, there's a dream, refusing closure. For Jacob, the tangible body is unseen, but the unseen dream seems tangible.

SECTION V: BEING SENT

chapter fifteen

INJUSTICE!

Then his brothers went to feed their father's flock in Shechem.

—Genesis 37:12

The event we are about to consider happened a significant amount of time after Joseph's dreams. We don't have a detailed timeline of the life of Joseph. However the text here conveys a pause in the dynamics between Joseph and his elder brothers. There's a silent, settling time. A period of quiet. A clock is ticking, however, and time is not healing the brothers.

Chapter 33:18 tells us that, after the tension of Jacob's meeting with Esau, he and his family went safely, or peacefully, to Shechem. This was a pleasant moment in what seems like a life peppered with problems. Here in Genesis 37:12 the brothers found themselves in Shechem again. There were healthy, lush pastures there.

The sense of peace and safety they experienced on their previous visit to Shechem would undoubtedly come back to them as they entered the city.

Being in Shechem should have relaxed them, enabling a natural redressing of attitudes and reactions to past events. It's often true that time heals. Rest is supposed to reform us as well as refresh us. What we see, as the story unfolds, is that the quiet peace of Shechem didn't unwind their hatred. If it had any effect on them it was to unwind their self-control. They were relaxing their guard against evil. They were using the quiet, the rest, to just swim with the tide of their worst emotions. If they had let things go, they were now letting them all come back again. The rise of this returning tide would determine Joseph's future, Jacob's future, and theirs.

So they came back to Shechem, where they had been before. When you find yourself back where you have been before, ask the Lord if you have something to learn that you should have learned the first time, and make sure you learn it this time!

They have left the cautious environment of home and are less restrained and therefore free to give vent to their bad feelings about their brother. On hillsides night by night, together, in the name of fellowship around the campfire, they exploit each other's weaknesses to enflame their own. Their returning hatred will use injustice to justify injustice—the murder of an innocent. They are without doubt the fathers of the Pharisees!

Injustice, real or imagined, can give us a sense of righteous indignation, even when we are soaked in iniquity ourselves, and our rage is totally disproportionate to the problem (a dream)! Still we feel a sense of righteous justification for any act of revenge.

There's nothing like a sense of injustice—a feeling of being unfairly treated, real or imagined, in a family or in a nation—to unite men and women. It's powerful enough to raise family against family and nation against nation. Here it was brother against brother—the worst kind of war; who called it "civil"?

The brothers were on the hillsides on beautiful balmy nights, with sheep safely in the fold. Whiling away the hours, they clouded the clear starry sky and polluted the clean night air with murderous profanity. We are saddened to assume this, but, as Joseph dreamily approached them, with concern for their welfare, food, and good things from his father and theirs, they instantly proposed murder! He merely dreamed; they were wide awake to execute!

They didn't arrive at this position without preparation. And all on beautiful pastoral hills. It's not surprising when we discover, as Joseph did, that they had left Shechem, the place of safety, and moved to Dothan.

chapter sixteen

SENIOR THINGS

And Israel said to Joseph, "Are not your brothers feeding the flock in Shechem?"

—Genesis 37:13

By this point in the narrative Jacob begins to look like an old man. Has age caught up? Is he getting quiet and uninterested in life? Is he not sure exactly where the other brothers are? Perhaps he doesn't care much. It could be that he has had a moment of conscience, reminding him how long it has been since he last checked. So he feels he should get an update.

Jacob is getting old, but what we are seeing is not simply aging. What we are beginning to see is a senior who used to walk with God, now buried in himself and his family pain. He's a senior whose focus has shifted; his energy has gone inward, his mind taken up with private issues. God has all but gone! This picture increases as the story unfolds. Jacob, Israel, the prince with God, has grown cold to the Lord. The passive heaviness that comes across in the language used to describe Jacob is spiritually telling!

He has lost a long-time friend in the death of Rebekah's nurse (Genesis 35:8). He has lost his much loved wife Rachel (Genesis 35:19). He's tired of his sons' failures and disputes, and he would like it to all go away and leave him alone. He would possibly like to have Joseph and Benjamin remain with him. But then, as now, life wisely doesn't let us choose.

"Come, I will send you to them" (Genesis 37:13). In this verse Jacob sends Joseph. Perhaps a moment of his former self moves him

to reach out to his other sons. However, if Jacob is getting a bit old, God uses it to further His purposes. He lets Jacob send Joseph on a mercy mission. How many disastrous decisions are made in careless moments! When preparing to meet Esau, Jacob at least sensed the danger! Not so here. He sends his favourite child into the wilderness to find a group of hostile brothers and has no caution; no alarms are sounding in his heart or head. He can't see the danger.

chapter seventeen
COME AND GO

He says to Joseph, "*Come.*" The invitation to come is always a beautiful moment, isn't it? Jesus said, when addressing the weary and heavily laden, "*Come to Me, all you who labor and are heavy laden, and I will give you rest*" (Matthew 11:28). In the book of Revelation, "*the Spirit and the bride say, 'Come!'*" (Revelation 22:17). Such a warm invitation to a moment of cherished closeness, undoubtedly a beautiful moment!

God has given you such an invitation to come. He has issued it to *you*. It has remained where He placed it in the book of Isaiah for you to see and read and hear in your heart. "'*Come now, and let us reason together,' Says the LORD, 'Though your sins are like scarlet, They shall be as white as snow; Though they are red like crimson, They shall be as wool'*" (Isaiah 1:18). The invitation, this call, is not to heaven—yet! It's a call to come to the Lord and be cleansed and filled and made useful for His service, to be sent out as an ambassador for His Son into a hostile world, just like Joseph here. This invitation to come close to the Lord, this passionate calling to intimate conversation—have you known it? Many have, down countless ages, men, women, and children from all of humanity, all defined by our one common name: "sinners."

But notice that Jacob's invitation to come near is quickly followed by a breaking of that closeness. It says, "*Come, I will send you to them*" (Genesis 37:13). And, like many a pastor, he's sent to hostile brethren.

The present-day Christian church often presents an image of a church that loves this beautiful moment of coming to Jesus. But it reveals a strict and particular resistance to the call to "go." It refuses to leave the wonderful place of communion and worship and take up the self-sacrifice of being sent.

These words *"Come, I will send you"* are said to all of us who come to Jesus. We are to come, and go. Come to Jesus, then go into all the world and be His witnesses so that the lost might be found among men.

Jacob will send Joseph to a particular group—his brothers. Likewise the Lord sends us to find the lost members of His elect family, those chosen before the foundation of the world. Where are they? We don't know; we are just to go and proclaim the word of life, and they will respond when they hear that word, the message of the gospel. Jesus said, *"My sheep hear My voice"* (John 10:27). No amount of worship will bring them to Jesus; only the spoken word of the gospel will give life to the dead, salvation to men.

Is this a call to some kind of paid employment? Not really, though Jacob did provide for Joseph's journey, indicating that God will provide all our needs. This is the basic invitation and command of the Lord to all believers. We are to go into all the world and preach the gospel.

chapter eighteen

THE PRAYER MEETING

Then he said to him, "Please go and see if it is well with your brothers and well with the flocks, and bring back word to me."

—Genesis 37:14

The message of the gospel deals with us and everything that concerns us. The brothers and their flocks make a complete picture here. Joseph must see if it is well with both.

Israel is clearly feeling the need to reach out to his sons. They are far away from him. Surely God in His great heart longs to reach out to us. Hear the words of Jesus: *"O Jerusalem, Jerusalem...How often I wanted to gather your children together...but you were not willing!"* (Matthew 23:37). This gathering relates to all that concerns us and our "flocks."

So Israel sends Joseph to go and find his brothers. While in this world, believers have this as a continual mission—to search out, wherever we are, the children of God and *"see if it is well with"* them. Having met them and asked about their lives and souls, we are to return to the Lord and bring a report. Surely this is a picture of true prayer: to take the time to find God's children wherever we go, to get to know them, to learn the state of their souls, and to then return to the place of prayer and raise them up before God for blessing or help. How much fuel for prayer before the throne of grace should this give us? What a prayer meeting that would be!

Jacob's immediate concern is for the brothers themselves and then for their flocks. The needs of the brothers and their flocks indicate a set of priorities. First the brothers themselves; then their flocks. We are allowed to see a parallel here in the spiritual needs of their souls and the physical needs that surround them. We know from the attitudes they show towards their brother that they are far away from God. We know that they are in great need of spiritual awakening.

This sense of priority of needs is often reversed in church prayer meetings. God's concern for us is first for our souls. Members typically focus on one physical ailment after the next without pause or silence, running through the lists of patients and progress. But they don't know if the person sitting beside them on a Sunday morning is going to heaven or hell!

Do you hear the medical knowledge that has been learned in the church community? Just listen to our prayers; we discuss bloodwork with God. We show chemical values and diagnostics that medical students wish they had grasped! God is the great Physician, always has been! But today one might think He has laid aside His pastoral rod and staff for a stethoscope. He no longer has a flock on the hillsides of this wicked world; they all seem to be in the local hospital struggling to get out of bed.

God's interests, it seems from the content of today's prayer meetings, have decidedly shifted in just a few decades. We will pray for physical healing for the unbeliever and not ever mention his soul, lost in trespasses and sins. He's bound for a lost eternity in hell, but at least we prayed for his broken leg!

Imagine Paul and Peter at the Jerusalem counsel, discussing their blood chemistry, their diets, the diagnosis of their members, their pains, their discomforts. No! No! No! These things were of only marginal interest. After all, they might have been thrown into jail the next day or fed to lions. Paul's brief mention of his pains would have turned the Bible into a medical textbook if he were as physical in his interests as we have become! What would his medical description have been, having been left for dead or sunk in the sea for days? Oh the indulgence it would be given at a prayer meeting today! Such an opportunity to show our knowledge, our amateur

The Prayer Meeting

medical skills. We will pray for anything other than a man's soul to be saved. Our prayers are bereft of spiritual understanding; they have little spiritual passion! What have we allowed ourselves to become, dear reader?

Suggest in a prayer meeting that, having just finished the medical round, we concentrate for the second half of the time on lost souls, even lost souls in our families—silence ensues! Confusion in the ranks and an angry sense of downright indignation! But why is that so often the case? Why is there no pleading with God? Why is there no explanation in the presence of God as to the spiritual illness facing sinners? Why is there no urgency for real answers? Why no impatience expressed for spiritual healing of backsliders? Why above all no continued discussion after the meeting closes about souls instead of endless talk of rotting physical frames? Such energy misspent on the carcass that is dying as soon as it's born, which we seem to be afraid to talk about in prayer. Such a lack of knowledge about essential spiritual conditions, and such intense interest in "tents." Paul disparagingly referred to his body to as *"this tent"* (2 Corinthians 5:1), which he longed to be out of but we love! Who replaced spirituality in prayer with practicality? Who convinced us that a man's body required more prayer than his soul? They did us a severe disservice!

Joseph must bring a report about the flocks, but only after he has reported and explained and related all about the brothers themselves to their father.

Joseph will find his brothers and be concerned for all that affects them. He will bring them supplies for their bodies. But he will especially bring news from their father, whom they have not spoken to in a long time. He should meet them at Shechem, but he will discover they have moved away. Joseph will not give up until he finds them, but when he does, they will decide to kill him, and he's only seventeen!

"So he sent him out of the Valley of Hebron, and he went to Shechem" (Genesis 37:14). Joseph was sent out of Hebron, to go to Shechem. The name *Hebron*, the place Joseph was leaving, suggests gathering together or perhaps grouping together. It was in a valley,

so it's called the *"vale of Hebron"* in some Bible translations. Joseph was leaving the place of companionship and friendship to go to find his brothers, who should be his friends, but they are not at this point in time. He went to Shechem, north of Hebron. He didn't find his brothers where their father said they should be; they had wandered far away, just like we may have.

chapter nineteen

THINGS OF THE SPIRIT

Now a certain man found him, and there he was, wandering in the field. And the man asked him, saying, "What are you seeking?"

—Genesis 37:15

Joseph was seeking his brothers but didn't find them. Joseph was wandering, the Bible says, *"in the field,"* not "in *a* field," suggesting that he was in the right field, the field he had been sent to. You can see him looking at the field and saying, "They should be here!" He wandered around in the field, looking up this valley and round that hill and along the stream bed. Having exhausted all the routes, he was still wandering aimlessly around the field, the right field.

Did you ever feel this aimless sense in your Christian walk? You're in the place where you know God wants you to be, you haven't forgotten your calling to that field, but something is missing! You can't find what you're looking for. So long have you tried that you have lost your way. Your days are best described as aimless, directionless, well-nigh pointless, but you know why you are there. That's when God sends "a certain man." He finds you. You're the one looking for others, but you have to be found yourself. Who is this man?

The man finds Joseph wandering. The wording has an air of searching about it; perhaps he's looking for Joseph. He asks Joseph, *"What are you seeking?"* The answer will tell him if Joseph has lost his sense of calling. If he's looking for his brethren, he is Joseph and still obedient. If not, Joseph is not who this man is looking for. Or he will need to do a work in Joseph before he sends him on his way rejoicing to find the brethren again. But Joseph is still searching and has not lost his calling here.

This *"man"*—who is he? We aren't told. However this brief meeting reminds me of others in the Old Testament that are interpreted by many as brief appearances of God the Holy Spirit. He comes and goes without introduction. The texts leave us wishing we knew more about him!

The passages where the Holy Spirit appears in the Old Testament leave us guessing until the New Testament reveals him as the third person of the Trinity, God the Holy Spirit! He's still going about this world, taking care of God's people. *If* this is another appearance of the Holy Spirit, He takes Joseph, whom He has been tracking to keep safe, and He redirects him to find his brothers, whom He has also been keeping track of, thus guiding and smoothing the workings of God in the world and fulfilling His purposes.

> *So he [Joseph] said, "I am seeking my brothers. Please tell me where they are feeding their flocks." And the man said, "They have departed from here, for I heard them say, 'Let us go to Dothan.'" So Joseph went after his brothers and found them in Dothan.*
>
> —Genesis 37:16–17

So here we (perhaps!) have the Holy Spirit. He has been listening to the brothers' conversation, knows all about their hateful intentions, yet sends Joseph to where they are. God's ways are past finding out. The brothers will not get away from God the Holy Spirit! God even calls Jacob's elderly frailty to His service as he carelessly sends Joseph to the brothers, alone—but he wasn't alone, was he?

Joseph goes to Dothan, thirteen miles (twenty kms) north of Shechem. Dothan was on the major trade route to Egypt. It wasn't a great trade centre; it just was on the route. The name *Dothan* means "two wells." We might think it would be a place of refreshment. Perhaps it was for the brothers, but not for Joseph. Sometimes those places in life with the most promise turn out to be the places of the most pain. Then again it could indicate two groups gathering at different wells in the same small town...I think we have all seen this strange phenomena! A tiny little town in the country and two churches that split a century ago! They are still drinking at separate wells every Sunday!

In the story of Joseph we certainly have one family and two wells, but the two wells are different kind of water. Joseph is drinking at a pure river of the water of life, the brothers from a well they contaminated for themselves long ago. Joseph finds them at Dothan, which is an interesting place from a geographical perspective.

So where is Dothan? The brothers travelled pretty well due north from Hebron to Shechem, then north again with a slight bend westwards as they went. So Dothan basically lay northwest of Shechem. Joseph followed on the same route but with a time delay caused by the thirteen-mile walk. He would probably arrive at Dothan the same day that he met the man.

The Ishmaelite traders were north of Dothan, travelling southwest. They would pass through Dothan, heading south to the Nile Valley in Egypt. All of them would arrive in perfect time.

The brothers arrived first, and Joseph's arrival was divinely timed for that moment when they had reached some agreement as to what they intended to do to him should the opportunity arise. The Midianite traders would arrive a short time later when the brothers had decided not to kill Joseph but not yet what they would do with him. Each group imagined the meeting to be a chance happening.

So the brothers arrived in Dothan first, followed by Joseph, and they crossed paths with the Ishmaelite traders who were travelling in the opposite direction, all guided by the Holy Spirit but imagining they were all doing their own thing. God's timing is perfect!

And so Joseph finds his brothers and walks towards them with the same innocence as he had sharing his dreams with them. Maybe he has even forgotten his dreams! But the brothers live on those dreams. Jacob also had them in mind, and God was working them out to reality!

SECTION VI:
WITHOUT DOUBT

chapter twenty

RENAMING THINGS

Now when they saw him afar off, even before he came near them, they conspired against him to kill him. Then they said to one another, "Look, this dreamer is coming! Come therefore, let us now kill him and cast him into some pit; and we shall say, 'Some wild beast has devoured him.' We shall see what will become of his dreams!"
—Genesis 37:18–20

Jacob said to Joseph, *"Come, I will send you"* (Genesis 37:13). The brothers said to each other, *"Come…let us now kill him."*
The goal they have been working towards for years is nearing them, at a pace. The details are instantly decided—the pit, the wild beast. All this to *"see what will become of his dreams!"* Committing murder to kill off dreams? Ten grown men. Their great-grandfather is Abraham. Their grandfather is Isaac; their father is Jacob. They were brought up to fear the Lord God of their fathers. Their mothers nursed them on godly principles; they know about Adam and Eve, Cain and Abel, and Sodom. They began life with lively consciences. Ten of them together now conspire to murder their younger brother over his dreams. How quickly men fall! How long are the centuries that produce civilizations of note, yet how short is the distance between that sophisticated civilized society and brutal madness. They will see what will become of his dreams, but not as they expect and not for a long time, during which they will be brought to nothing. *"For when Your judgments are in the earth, The inhabitants of the world will learn righteousness"* (Isaiah 26:9).

There are some telling things that show us what had developed. So here we have the brothers sitting around chatting about Joseph, conspiring to kill him. There's a fellowship in this conspiring. Agreement is reached in a moment—hatred only needs a moment. Hatred being incoherent, the matter is spontaneously summed up without the confusion of deliberating facts. They sum up and conclude, spontaneously giving Joseph a new name. They call him *"this dreamer."* He is now the dreamer.

It took years to come. Gradually, night by night, imperceptibly, they arrived at this position. Now they will execute their intention. This is not a rational event. The accusers have spent more time fantasizing than Joseph, who only dreamed two dreams! They condemn themselves as they mete out the punishment: *"Let us now kill him."* Nature's public gallery gasps, affirming that their intention to kill him was an outrageous injustice!

They have given him a new name! That blessed name *Joseph*, that exuberant declaration of God's goodness, has been replaced. They have reduced Joseph to *"this dreamer"*!

In the Genesis narrative the brothers never address him as Joseph. Hatred of someone makes it difficult for us to call the person by their name. How comfortable are you referring to someone by their first name? Here in this moment the brothers find the ability to address him by name—not by his true name, Joseph, but by a name that comfortably slips off their fiery tongues, lubricated by the devouring enzymes of hatred. It's the opposite of what was conferred by Rachel. She expanded her son as far as her loving maternal soul could; she called him "God will add." They reduced him to the *"dreamer."*

He merely dreamed! How was it that they couldn't see this way back in time when they were so angry over his dreams? Why didn't they just ignore his dreams as the flimsy things they were? It was because the human heart has a truth indicator. Joseph's dreams were truth! His brothers felt the force of truth and rejected it, instantly. How convoluted are our emotions; how complicated we are, how arrogantly confused! We are arrogant even when we are knowingly confused. Our confusion should produce a humility, but it doesn't.

Joseph means nothing to them. They might have written the account beginning "Joseph, being nothing." As long as we see someone as a person with real value, it's difficult for us to dismiss them, let alone kill them. We must first dehumanize our enemies. This enables us to silence the screaming accusations of our conscience that raise an awful alarm when we are about to quench a life.

The brothers knew what they would do, perhaps only fantasizing how it could ever happen. Then one day, they looked out across the plain below the hillside, and behold, there he was, walking towards them! How did they recognize him while he was a long way off? By a coat! An instantly recognizable coat identified him among the verdant pastures, which were more lush and welcoming, more fertile, than Shechem, according to the experts. That coat declared him their father's favourite son, and that salt in their wound made Joseph's death instantly more palatable, indeed instantly desirable!

Be careful what you talk about; be careful about indulging your fantasies. Every time we indulge a fantasy it weakens our ability to resist the reality, should it present itself! The reality, the possibility to actually kill Joseph, presented itself as though by a miracle. Many things happen to us, and the timing is the essential key that opens the door to good or evil. Now the time is right, even though it's all wrong!

chapter twenty-one

FANTASY

Did the brothers realize that dreaming about killing Joseph night after night together, over long periods of time, exploring the best way, the easiest way, the safest way, to do the deed would make it easier for them to do the actual deed when the possibility arose?

Our world today is filled with fantasy. Our youth are not allowed innocent dreams; they must be killing people. Destruction and violence are their daily mental diet. The fact that it's mere fantasy doesn't lessen its danger. This excessive amount of fantasy has made them immune to suffering, immune to destruction, immune to pain, immune to ugliness and to evil itself.

This age is saturated with pastimes that every other generation would have condemned. But to us, it's just entertainment, to while away the hours and days and years. But one day, if a real opportunity comes and the timing is right, a terrible, inexplicable event may occur! Yet still we refuse to give up our pastimes! We are almost numb to tragedy if it's presented to us on a screen. We may even be more interested in the advertisement following fast behind a news story of a tragedy. By the next news story, we've forgotten the previous one, no matter how bad. Where is the wisdom of watching world events while easing your mind into an evening's relaxation with your children? How mixed up are we as a society? We are scarily similar to Joseph's siblings.

chapter twenty-two

REUBEN

So it came to pass, when Joseph had come to his brothers, that they stripped Joseph of his tunic, the tunic of many colors that was on him.

—Genesis 37:23

"*So it came to pass.*" This is a simple, seemingly innocent start to this section. Yet the thing that came to pass is horrendous! Ten adult older brothers overcame their younger brother. Fought him to subjection. Stripped his outer coat off him and threw him into a pit so deep he could not escape from it. They then discussed the method of his death while they ate supper! How terrible a moment was this! It nevertheless *"came to pass."* They didn't find it difficult to do, because they had been rehearsing it for years as they watched the flocks on the hillsides.

"*Then they took him and cast him into a pit. And the pit was empty; there was no water in it*" (Genesis 37:24). He was going to die in that pit one way or another unless Reuben came back on time. Reuben didn't come back on time! How many years did he relive that moment? How many self-examinations did he undertake? Did he think that God was punishing him for his affair with his father's concubine? How many times did he say "If only…"? When troubles came for him in later life, did he remember this failure and think he was being punished by God?

God made Reuben late in order to enable Joseph to both live and get to Egypt. Sometimes God can take the blame; He's big enough to handle it! When you hear the accuser's voice about the past, remember that God has forgotten your past sins. If you're a believer, your sins have been washed away by the blood of Christ, and you have been forgiven. God has forgotten your sins; don't let the devil remind you of them!

Here is a picture of the Son of God in the hands of sinful men. He came from Heaven to earth to seek us out for the Father. Without cause we took Him and stripped Him of His coat, and we crucified Him. We put Him to death for no cause other than that *"We will not have this man to reign over us"* (Luke 19:14).

chapter twenty-three

SELLING THINGS

Then they lifted their eyes and looked, and there was a company of Ishmaelites, coming from Gilead with their camels.
—Genesis 37:25

Isn't life often this way for us? An apparently chance meeting results in a joint blessing, a new job, a new friend, a new church, whatever. Look for His hand and acknowledge His work in your life, even in the bad times. See Him, and everything becomes worthwhile. If you ignore this principle, life can be very hard and rob you of the thrill of being a part of what God is doing.

Unfortunately, Joseph's brothers are not looking for God. They are alert for evil.

So Judah said to his brothers, "What profit is there if we kill our brother and conceal his blood? Come and let us sell him to the Ishmaelites, and let not our hand be upon him, for he is our brother and our flesh." And his brothers listened. Then Midianite traders passed by; so the brothers pulled Joseph up and lifted him out of the pit, and sold him to the Ishmaelites for twenty shekels of silver.
—Genesis 37:26–28

Judah comes to the rescue in the absence of Reuben. The traders are called Ishmaelites first, because of their descent from Ishmael, and then Midianites, because they came from the land of Midian. They were wild men, expert with a bow and rough but carrying luxuries to Egypt. Joseph was sold to them for twenty shekels of silver, less than Jesus was sold for but close enough to remind us, as we read, that the Lord Jesus, the Son of God incarnate, was sold for just thirty pieces of silver.

How do you value Him who gave His all for you? How does your valuation translate in financial terms? We are exposed so often, as the brothers were, without realizing it. Our charitable giving in church very often exposes our valuation of that church. And we generally don't even realize that we have just expressed a valuation of something. The brothers here put a value on Joseph like the chief priest put a value on Jesus, and too often we do as well at the offering time. We wonder why the Lord's presence is not as it should be in the worship service. It may not be the pastor's or the worship team's fault; it's just as likely that low offering numbers are at fault!

chapter twenty-four

SWEET THINGS

And they took Joseph to Egypt.

—Genesis 37:28

So, in what seems like no time at all, it's all easily executed. No problem—it's done.

Genesis 37:25 says the caravan was *"bearing spices, balm, and myrrh, on their way to carry them down to Egypt."* Joseph was no doubt roughly thrown among these items. Imagine this journey. He had walked for a long time to find his brothers, then was stripped and thrown into a pit for another length of time. Now he was sitting on a camel or in the back of a wagon laden with bags of spices, balm, and myrrh! At worst he was tied to a camel and walking in the heat of the day. But God is good, and perhaps Joseph sensed His gracious presence all the way through the sweet aroma from the spices. The Hebrew word translated "spices" refers to anything having a pleasant odour, usually herbs. Balm was used as an ointment for healing wounds. The myrrh of the Old Testament is not the same as the myrrh of the New Testament. The Old Testament myrrh was a shrub called rockrose. It grows in rocks and sand and produces a perfumed gum.[5] Spices, balm, and myrrh are interesting because suffering is a major theme in this story about Joseph. But there was a contradictory sweetness in the air from the spices, creating a poignant picture of the ointment poured over Jesus' head and remaining with him all the way to the cross. In Jesus' case, it symbolized

---

5 Merrill C. Tenney, ed., *Zondervan's Pictorial Bible Dictionary* (n.p.: Zondervan, 1967), 665.

the worshipful aspect of suffering accepted submissively as from His Father. That's true also of Joseph here. One might wonder if a little balm might have been acquired to sooth any wounds acquired on the journey or lingering from the scuffle when the brothers threw Joseph into the pit. The myrrh may have reminded him that beauty can arise from barren rocks and dry sand.

In every bare or hard place we can elect to let our suffering feed the beauty of patience and perseverance, or we can refuse to let it reach us and grow deeper in our bitterness against God and men or life itself. Bitterness makes us ugly and miserable instead of blooming like beautiful roses, even if on barren rocks. What have you chosen? Joseph remained the same person all the way through this journey.

God always sends us sweet simple comforts, not to be ignored for their simplicity. Submission and cheerful acceptance of the providence of God sends forth a sweet-smelling incense that rises all the way to heaven. In Joseph's case, and many others, it still lingers, and we sense it while reading his story, even in the 21st century!

chapter twenty-five

WHERE SHALL I GO?

Then Reuben returned to the pit, and indeed Joseph was not in the pit; and he tore his clothes. And he returned to his brothers and said, "The lad is no more; and I, where shall I go?"

—Genesis 37:29–30

Reuben has yet another failure to add to his list. He almost helped! Almost was not good enough. But God causes *"all things [to] work together for good to those who love God, to those who are the called according to His purpose"* (Romans 8:28).

Reuben asked, *"Where shall I go?"* It appears that the brothers hadn't told Reuben what they did. He assumed that Joseph was dead: *"The lad is no more."* Is it possible that this was the beginning of a disintegration among the brothers? They gave Jacob an agreed-upon simple explanation for what happened to Joseph, but as time passed and questions arose or conversations occurred at home that threatened to expose them, could it be that their relationship began to break down and they feared that one or another might tell Jacob the truth? This is what often happens to partners in crime; they expose each other and become arch enemies.

"They took Joseph's tunic, killed a kid of the goats, and dipped the tunic in the blood" (Genesis 37:31). It must have been a beautiful coat. These men take this coat, created by their own father's heart, and dip it and smear it and spoil it with the blood of an animal. This is how little we care about the hearts of others when we want something.

They were no better off with Joseph gone. He hadn't dreamed in a long time, or at least he hadn't talked to them about dreams in a long time. He wasn't doing anything anymore to irritate them; he was simply living. If they couldn't kill him they would create a fantasy that they could even believe themselves.

> *Then they sent the tunic of many colors, and they brought it to their father and said, "We have found this. Do you know whether it is your son's tunic or not?"*
> —Genesis 37:32

One lie leads to another. Often the initial event is overshadowed by the later events required to patch things up. Note the language: *"your son,"* not *"our brother."* When we have a guilty conscience we use our language skills to ease ourselves in our guilt. *"And he recognized it and said, 'It is my son's tunic. A wild beast has devoured him'"* (Genesis 37:33). How unwittingly Jacob declares an awful truth about mankind! These brothers have stooped to the level of being animalistic. They have in effect devoured Joseph. In their hearts they would have allowed wild animals to savage him. How far man, made in the image of God, can fall! And Jacob declares it.

chapter twenty-six

WITHOUT DOUBT

"Without doubt Joseph is torn to pieces."

—Genesis 37:33

Without doubt: the evidence is irrefutable. The case is sound; there's no other way to look at it. It is *"without doubt."* Yet Joseph is alive!

How many times have we seen what looks to be without doubt true accepted as evidence against God or His Word or His church? Why is our faith so weak?

We may not know what's wrong, but something is wrong, and it's not God or His Word. When doubt raises its ugly head we should put it down and not indulge or sanctify it. We should never spread our doubts, never make a show of them. *"Let patience have its perfect work"* (James 1:4). We don't get all the answers in this life. We will not need them in the next!

Certainly the drama we are about to watch is based on fake evidence. It's a prefabricated case, not true to what actually happened. This isn't unusual in the affairs of men. Scientists are not perfect.

"Then Jacob tore his clothes, put sackcloth on his waist, and mourned for his son many days" (Genesis 37:34). The man of God believes a lie and publicly mourns Joseph, who is very much alive. Instantly the group follows the leader without a fight! Nobody looks at the evidence; nobody questions the brothers as to details; everyone accepts the obvious!

Being Joseph

And all his sons and all his daughters arose to comfort him; but he refused to be comforted, and he said, "For I shall go down into the grave to my son in mourning." Thus his father wept for him.

—Genesis 37:35

So many Christian churches are the same as this family. They are corporately mourning. They have no joy. They have no ability to witness verbally, because they have nothing to say that is convincing, because they have believed that "Joseph" is dead! They are afraid to speak because—like Joseph's wider family in their genuine grief over Joseph's apparent death—they believe their God is dead. This is the corporate image of religion: Joseph is dead; God is dead!

They say that they believe in God. But while the backslider is terrified of mere men, he strangely enough is not afraid of God. If he was, he would return in repentance and give up his defiance and his carping at God for not behaving like he thinks He should! Nevertheless, from this cold mechanical statement his experience and his understanding go down, down, down, into a deep empty cavern. So dark a place is religion as to defy investigation. It must be protected by impenetrable religious cordons. In this respect many departments of Christendom reveal that they are no more than empty ecclesiastical space. They hope to be in heaven one day. If they get there, they will get such an awakening to see Him all powerful and ruling in all the affairs of men!

Joseph is *alive*! But nobody seems to know it! How is this?

What's wrong here? Someone is telling lies, just like Joseph's brothers were, saying he was dead when he was not dead! That's what's wrong. There can be no joy until that lie is rejected and truth is believed by faith. Such a challenge faces the Christian individual and the Christian church today.

Sometimes God has to come to the individual and to whole church groups and pour out His Spirit upon them and open their eyes and fill them with life again. When it happens, everybody sees the change, and only the devil and his blind followers are unhappy.

Even the world senses something deep inside that is good. They may or may not recognize it as a sense of hope in the gospel, but many people take hope from the existence of the church. It gives them hope for a better future. Only a Spirit-filled church can do that. God gives you and me the oil of gladness and takes away our tears because Jesus is *alive*! Do not believe lies. Be "without doubt."

chapter twenty-seven

JUDAH AND TAMAR

Genesis 38:1-27

We leave Jacob mourning with all his family. They imagine Joseph to be thoroughly dead, but he is in fact thoroughly alive and travelling for the next few months, maybe half a year, to Egypt. The story is at a suitable point to break off and tell us about Judah. Judah might be seen as going into moral slavery as Joseph's journey takes him into physical slavery. Joseph and Judah are both on journeys at approximately the same time.

For us the shift from Joseph to Judah is a bit sudden. We've been so deeply connected with Joseph, and suddenly he has disappeared, out of sight and out of mind! The change doesn't seem like a wholesome advance in the narrative! Is this story misplaced? Some say it is! The question arises as we set out to read the history of Jacob and realize the narrative is going to be about Joseph. Here, we expect to follow Joseph into Egypt, but instead we are again surprised to find the story returning to Canaan and to Judah. Almost before we realize it, we are submerged with Judah and Tamar!

But the story in Genesis 38 is not as disconnected from the content in chapter 37 and 39 as it initially appears to be. It's not unrelated! It's not an isolated insertion as though some editor made a mistake. The story doesn't have to flow according to our hermeneutical demands. It has a pattern all of its own. The Bible is telling a spiritual story, not giving a mere history lesson.

So what is this story about, and how does it relate to Joseph and Jacob, whose history this is? It's told with characteristic Old

Testament freedom of speech and liberty of expression, yet all encapsulated within the dignity of God's inspired Word. What's it doing here? Let's see.

The last verse of Genesis 37 says, "*Now the Midianites had sold him [Joseph] in Egypt to Potiphar, an officer of Pharaoh and captain of the guard*" (Genesis 37:36). Then chapter 38 begins, "*It came to pass at that time that Judah departed from his brothers*" (Genesis 38:1). The story of Judah and Tamar then unfolds. Why the time connection? What is the relevance of this time between Joseph and Judah and between Judah and his brothers? When the Scriptures note the timing of events, we should note them too!

What time are we are to look at? This is the time between Joseph being sold to the Midianites and his journey to Egypt and being sold into Potiphar's household. This would be a significant length of time. Not years but certainly months, at the end of which Judah left his brothers. Let's say six months have passed while Joseph travelled to Egypt. So what?

It's first a simple matter of chronological fact. It's also likely that something significant happened between Judah and the other brothers during these months. Something happened that caused him to leave them. The timing is significant. As Joseph arrives in Potiphar's house in Egypt, Judah separates from his brethren in Canaan.

During those six months, the brothers had some time to talk. They were guilty of a serious set of offences and carried a lot of guilt. Such guilt among men can destroy them. The sin that unites us today can divide us tomorrow. Sin has a habit of turning on us nastily! It separates men from God and men from each other.

Go back a little and see Judah's part in the sale of Joseph.

> *Judah said to his brothers, "What profit is there if we kill our brother and conceal his blood? Come and let us sell him to the Ishmaelites, and let not our hand be upon him, for he is our brother and our flesh."*
>
> —Genesis 37:26–27

Judah and Tamar

The brothers agree, and Joseph is sold. He isn't killed. They go home to live with very uneasy consciences. Their minds don't forget as quickly or as easily as they thought they would. Sin remains at their door. They are left to discover the effects of sin in each of their lives as it plays out.

Did they dispute each other's role in the event? Very likely. Did they begin to examine each other and talk about each other? "If it hadn't been for you...!" "It wasn't my idea." "We should confess." "Surely God will punish us!" "This is all my fault." All and more is very likely to have swirled around home and the flocks on hillsides over these six months.

Did Judah have a softer heart? Did he become discouraged at the place he was in spiritually? Did he stop talking to his brothers? Chapter 38 tells us that he met a Canaanite called Hirah, and they became friends. He married a Canaanite woman and had children.

Then his life really gets complicated. This isn't always a sign that the Lord isn't with you but *is* always a time to sit down and take stock, to evaluate your life in every way. Judah chooses Tamar for his son Er, who is so wicked that God kills him. Judah gives Tamar to his other son Onan to raise an heir for his dead brother, as the practice was in those days. Onan cheats her so as not to give her a son, and God kills him for this wicked act. What a disaster Judah is in! He promises Tamar his son Shelah when he comes of age, but he doesn't follow through. Tamar decides to expose this in a very painful and public way.

The Bible raises another situation affected by time, saying, *"in the process of time...the daughter of Shua, Judah's wife, died"* (Genesis 38:12). Soon after his mourning was complete, *"Judas was comforted"* (Genesis 38:12). Judah went to a place called Timnah to shear his sheep with his Canaanite friend Hirah.

On the way he sees a veiled woman. Judah thinks she's a prostitute. She's in fact Tamar, acting the part to get back at Judah for not giving her his son Shelah, who is now of age. Her ploy works, and she becomes pregnant by Judah. Judah gives her his cord and his staff and his signet as surety for a goat that he will deliver in payment for her services. Judah sends the goat with his friend, but Tamar can't be found.

What's wrong with Judah? What has happened to him? Look at Judah in relation to Joseph's rejection. Some say he wanted to let Joseph live just because he wanted to make money. *"What profit is there?"* he asked (Genesis 37:26). This is doubtful in the light of his following statement. *"Let not our hand be upon him, for he is our brother and our flesh"* (Genesis 37:27). This is almost certainly a term of affection, or at least recognition! It isn't a mere ploy. Judah is to be seen as caring for Joseph when he saves him from death, not trying to make money out of him. How does he come to fall to the level we find him at in chapter 38? How did this mess come about?

Hidden sin unacknowledged and not dealt with before God is a very deep cancer in the soul. Judah had partaken in a sin against his brother. Could it be that a sense of shame and defeat grew in the intervening months, and he was overtaken by guilt? Not knowing what he could do about it and not willing to speak to Jacob about it for fear of the consequences, he's seen here as a man falling apart. Quite possibly this is due to a burden of despair that overwhelmed him to the point where he lost all his moral strength. Judah was lost! This was all happening while Joseph was being taken care of by the Lord in Potiphar's house. Joseph advanced in Egyptian captivity while his brother fell apart in Canaan.

The moral of the story of Judah and Tamar is that sin is a destructive cancer that lingers long after it takes root. It soon strangles the life of the host, and ruin quickly approaches such a man unless he repents. The change of heart brought about by repentance will engage God with him again in a very significant way. The situation with Tamar was the moment when all of Judah's failings came to a head, and it looks like he may well have made a life-changing decision then and God accomplished in him the change of heart that was required.

Judah is found out. He responds well to being discovered! He responds perhaps like David in a later narrative when he's found out and humbly says, *"I have sinned"* (2 Samuel 12:13). Like the sinner

Judah and Tamar

in the temple praying *"God, be merciful to me a sinner!"* (Luke 18:13). Like Peter saying to Jesus in the fishing boat, *"Depart from me, for I am a sinful man, O Lord!"* (Luke 5:8). So it looks like Judah had wandered away from the Lord, and this may be the story of his return to Him.

Is there a purpose in the positioning of the story? Yes, because here we can see the journey of the two brothers compared and contrasted. Joseph is taken by Judah and sold, and God works grace into his life in Potiphar's house. Judah is brought to his knees by Tamar, and his evident repentance restores his private relationship with the Lord.

The timing of these events in the lives of two sons of Israel may well be the beginning of God bringing these brothers, separated by sins, together again. It begins with both of them finding their lives going very wrong, and from a position of despair they are brought to a new place with the Lord. And it's all happening at the same time! They are separated by sin, by physical distance, and by circumstances neither can fix. Yet God has already begun the changes that are needed to restore them. As Judah settles in to come to terms with his sin, Joseph likewise settles in to come to terms with captivity. God settles in, so to speak, to work a change of heart in both of them that will facilitate getting Jacob and his children down to Egypt.

Never give up when you are separated from your Christian brother by sin. Though it may take many years, God has not given up on him, so don't you give up on him. And God has not given up on you, so don't give up on yourself either! God was in control in the despair of Joseph and also in the despair of Judah. He intended to bring them together in His own good time.

When the Bible says, *"This is the history of Jacob. Joseph, being seventeen years old"* (Genesis 27:2), it also sets out to tell us the background of a broken family. Here is a picture of the family of God—the church—in its brokenness.

The Word of God is honest and realistic about the state of the families of His servants, but note how God often still blesses His servants who are so burdened. Often our expectations of the families of God's servants are unrealistically and unbiblically higher than we hold for ourselves.

SECTION VII:
EGYPT

chapter twenty-eight
EGYPT IN JOSEPH'S TIME

Joseph was in Egypt around the time of the Twelfth Dynasty. As a slave he would have had time to learn the language and grow in his understanding of the nation. On the long journey down to Egypt the Ishmaelite traders would have gotten to know Joseph and realize he was a quality youth of some character and education. They would know who to sell him to, which is probably why he was taken to the house of Potiphar, the captain of the guard.

chapter twenty-nine

A SUCCESSFUL MAN

Now Joseph had been taken down to Egypt. And Potiphar, an officer of Pharaoh, captain of the guard, an Egyptian, bought him from the Ishmaelites who had taken him down there.

—Genesis 39:1

At this moment in Joseph's life everything is wrong and bad and terrifying and awful. But he doesn't fail or fall or give up! He carries the believer's characteristic quiet confident faith that confuses the unbeliever. Remember here, Joseph had been "taken down." These words are heavy with symbolism carried right through the Old Testament Scriptures. Going "down to Egypt" was never a good thing for God's people. After the exodus, *"down to Egypt"* meant a return to slavery and the house of bondage in Egypt, the antithesis of Canaan, God's promised land. At this point that's all to come, but there's a hint of it here in this downward journey into Egypt. Joseph remains there for years, with no attempt being made to find him or free him. Ask yourself, What is your biggest complaint about your own life right now? We can learn something from the mindset of Joseph.

As a child of God, Joseph understood that he had to be able to accept things the way they were, sometimes without a fight, yet never giving up. Joseph instinctively knew that this resigned mind could ironically keep him sane, even strong, in times of suffering.

This timeless mindset embraces suffering as something to be soberly accepted. Suffering is to be recognized as a present reality.

It's the experience of millions all over the world most of the time, and they must cope.

We must view suffering as something that we can overcome while we are still burdened. The victory of faith generally begins in the secret place of the heart and mind. Faith frees us from the spirit of bondage long before external freedom is achieved, if achieved at all. Those who overcome the spiritual bondage of captivity expand their own life that has been compressed. Their victory bypasses suffering and issues hope. See Paul and Silas in the dungeon at midnight singing God's praises. Their chains fall off and the prison doors burst open after they lift their hearts up by faith to praise. These men are at liberty while still in a dungeon designed for despair, before their iron chains are removed. This possibility is open for every believer and for any who suffer unjustly.

This overcoming, fighting, yet resigning human spirit gives us an incredible sense of being one with all who suffer. When it is given opportunity, suffering unites when it should isolate. It strengthens when it should weaken. It fills with love when it should fill with hate. It makes us serious about days that are not in our power to control when we should not care about any days at all. This personal sense of being and the realization that we are part of a suffering humanity have raised up some of the world's finest people. The history of the Christian Church is abundant with towering examples. The ability to embrace suffering and overcome it is one of the most notable characteristics of human beings.

The Christian man has a better chance of success in dealing with suffering than the atheist has. Both have the same potential human ability, but the believer has an added conviction of God's help that increases his ability to cope. Hence history is replete with Christian saints, but atheism doesn't even have the concept! Saints are those who, among others things, suffered immensely yet overcame.

The man of real faith, the true believer, can embrace suffering as coming from God and therefore believes it will produce good in the short term and long term. See Joseph's silent response to his troubles. There's no record of any complaint or fight. If there were such things, the Scriptures consider them as not worthy of mention.

Joseph had the benefit of a real religious aspect to life, not some meaningless ritualistic humdrum but a real knowledge of God. He knew he was not left to the whim of some chaotic universe, but rather he was kept in the hand of a loving and all-powerful God, and nothing happened by uncontrollable "chance." God is in control, and bad things happen to believers. That's a fact!

Throughout the Bible we see suffering being accepted and made to work. Joseph was a suffering believer and a beacon of hope to all who suffer; even in rejection and slavery, he became not a miserable man or a hopeless man but a "successful man."

"*The LORD was with Joseph, and he was a successful man; and he was in the house of his master the Egyptian*" (Genesis 39:2). Joseph *"was a successful man,"* even in foreign slavery, *"and he was in the house of his master the Egyptian."* This is so contrary to expectations. Everybody expects disaster, misery, mental and physical anguish, and an end to a life of any worth. Death might even be preferred—well, at least in our minds! Death might often be preferred to life, but when people actually face death, they cling and clutch and struggle and spend money and mortgage houses just to stay alive another few months! When faced with the possibility of sudden death, atheists frequently pray, and welcome prayer from others, to the God they say they do not believe in! Death is only ever attractive in theory! What are pharmaceuticals if not the failed and desperate human industry against "death" in all its forms? What a tragedy it would have been for Joseph and the world if he had chosen suicide rather than foreign slavery! Thank you, Joseph; you give us hope!

We are so familiar with the story that we sense no surprise, but the facts before us are surprising! Joseph was not just *"successful."* *"He was a successful man"*—that is a much more comprehensive statement! It means he had arrived at a place of achievement respected among men, and it was accompanied with all the trappings of what men would call success. Yet he was still a slave in Egypt! So

Being Joseph

a moment can command our spirit, or our spirit can command a moment. Joseph took command. Joseph prevailed.

chapter thirty

THE LORD WAS WITH HIM

And his master saw that the LORD was with him and that the LORD made all he did to prosper in his hand. So Joseph found favor in his sight, and served him. Then he made him overseer of his house, and all that he had he put under his authority.

—Genesis 39:3–4

This well-worn Bible phrase is worth some thought: *"The LORD was with him."* What does the Bible mean when it uses such strange language? It indeed means just what it says. Those who seek Him find Him or are found by Him. They begin to have a sense of His presence with them. They know it, and others know it too. It often is accompanied with seasons of real blessing, but it can be there in the thick of trouble, giving them a solid confidence that's confusing to others. It's confusing because the believer is often seen as a weak person needing help from a deity. Often the believers themselves are quite surprised by the peace and sense of assurance they have. They cease to strive and struggle through life. They walk with a confident contentment. They carry themselves with a humble, open peace. They are a blessing to the righteous and draw the unrighteous to a better hope. There's generally someone they will irritate as well!

So it was, from the time that he had made him overseer of his house and all that he had, that the LORD blessed the

Being Joseph

Egyptian's house for Joseph's sake; and the blessing of the LORD was on all that he had in the house and in the field.
—Genesis 39:5

Not only are these believers blessed, but often all who favour them are also blessed, as is the case of Joseph in Potiphar's house. However, when the Lord is with us, we don't always do well! Some preach that doing well is guaranteed to the man walking with God. That is so untrue to the whole Scriptures, and it's shown in Joseph's life right up to this moment. Although all he does prospers, he's still a slave in a foreign land!

This sort of picture is common right to the end of the Bible. There we find the great and elderly apostle John. He is *"in the Spirit on the Lord's day"* (Revelation 1:10). But he's in exile on the island of Patmos at that very moment! The gospel is a long-term message. It promises us freedom from trouble and pain and sin ultimately in heaven. God does often bless His people, and sometimes, even when they are not close to Him, He still blesses people out of His magnificent mercy. Joseph, at this time despite his circumstances, is pleasing the Lord. He is blessed, and all he does prospers.

chapter thirty-one

JOSEPH, BEING HANDSOME

Thus he left all that he had in Joseph's hand, and he did not know what he had except for the bread which he ate. Now Joseph was handsome in form and appearance.
—Genesis 39:6

Why would God's Holy Word tell us such a seemingly irrelevant thing? It's out of character to raise such superficiality, such a downgrade from spiritual blessings, from God to the physical, let alone mere external looks, right here in the midst of blessing. Everything is going so well. God's blessing is being poured out on Joseph. At this point in the story it is real spiritual blessing. He is blessed; his master is blessed; what else is there to talk about right now? Amid all the abundance of blessing, even the threat that has just been declared to us is, in itself, a blessing from God. The threat is that now Joseph is handsome!

The sentence silently weaves a question into any mind that will receive it: "Why are You telling us this, Lord?" The Word of God says, *"Now Joseph was handsome in form and appearance."* This sentence serves a simple purpose. It gently startles us and takes us by surprise! It causes us to adjust our focus. We now thinly understand blessing. We think it's 100 percent good. It's always, we think, enjoyable and positive. This sentence should cause us to reconsider!

When an astronomer observes the moons of Jupiter and encounters the very faintest of the Jovian rings, the Thebe gossamer ring, he stops and clears his vision. There's a band around the moon, but it's not like the moon. There's a spoiling, a deterioration, at its edges. The obstruction is clear but not solid; it is in fact a band of celestial dust particles, but it causes him to refocus. It will produce a change in the astronomer's mindset, a shift away from its present fixation to something a little less substantial than the Jovian moon—celestial dust! But it will prompt a more intelligent, a more critical, view of things that look so solid.

We need something similarly gentle but equally surprising to reset our focus when we are engrossed with solid God-given spiritual blessings! The sentence *"Joseph was handsome"* does this for us. It stops us with a surprise, causing us to think. It prepares us for the disappointment about to come in the story of Joseph in Egypt. It brings us back a pace to a more real world. A world we know, a fallen world. There's a spoiling at the edges, betraying the insubstantial nature of the gossamer rings. *"Joseph was handsome"* is the spoiling of the edges in this story. But we read on, with a more grounded mind, as the story continues.

Nothing happens quickly. It's not sudden, but it starts soon after the blessing is firmly established and has the potential for long-term good. We kindly call it human frailty. The Bible spells it out as total depravity—not that all men are all bad all of the time but that all men are incapable of being all good all of the time. They may be very good lots of the time, especially when compared to each other. The sinner may often be better than the saint. All of us have a bias towards sin that spoils all we do. Even our righteousness is, in God's perfect sight, filthy rags (Isaiah 64:6)! Yet all the while we wear these filthy rags with self-righteous pride, imagining that we are as we see ourselves among ourselves.

The sentence *"Joseph was handsome"* is like the gossamer rings. It reminds us that blessings in this life will often be insubstantial. They will always be spoiled at the edges. Permanence and substance are only to be found in heaven. Our legitimate enjoyment of blessings must be held in control by such truths, but note that this spoiling is only at the edges of blessing.

The problem for Joseph was not simply a woman with a roving eye and a lack of self-control. The problem was Joseph's good looks. That is where the Bible begins this episode in his life. It doesn't begin by telling us that the woman was dangerous, although she certainly was! The Word of God is telling us that Joseph was dangerous! Here we have another good thing, a handsome appearance, spoiled! Just when everything was so good, the Bible brings us back to a tainted, frail world where we can't have what we want. Perfection is in heaven.

The churches' current obsession, current blessing even, good or bad in itself, is often the problem we can only mention gently, and perhaps not even by name. It may be named "celestial dust." We are not to be too taken by blessings. We are to be fully taken up by the one who blesses!

As a yacht tacks from side to side it crosses the ideal route to its destination—that is, the perfect straight line it can't achieve due to wind direction. It only touches the perfect place for a moment as it crosses over that invisible line. It's incapable of staying on that line for more than a brief moment. As soon as it gets to it, it passes it. So it is with men in every area where they think they have arrived at perfection. They have just sailed right past it. They only ever see it coming and watch it going. They can't hold it for long, except at their destination—heaven.

We need this critical examiner to be at work constantly, if gently. We need critics even in good times. Especially in good times, or we will lose them.

Potiphar laid aside his critical faculties regarding his home, his work, and, above all here, his wife. He had simply let go of everything and imagined that Joseph could make it work on his own. One way or another Potiphar did what an official in a royal household, let alone a married man, can never do! He "left all." He left all the overseeing of his own household to a slave. No doubt Joseph was doing things well. No doubt Potiphar had nothing to worry about. Joseph would do the right thing by him. But he forgot that the real, true nature of humanity is a corrupt fallen nature that always soils and spoils. It has a reverse Midas touch! *"Joseph was handsome"* is where even a blessing becomes dangerous.

Being Joseph

And it came to pass after these things that his master's wife cast longing eyes on Joseph, and she said, "Lie with me."

—Genesis 39:7

Oh, Joseph…if only you had been unattractive! There are such benefits to blandness! But the Scriptures tell us *"Joseph was handsome."* He was not just physically handsome but a beautiful person inside as well. A package seldom found, a prize combination, a rare jewel. This woman was attracted to this handsome man. She didn't resist.

The Bible says she *"cast longing eyes on Joseph."* We are back to fantasy again! She lay in bed at night, or sat in the palace by day, having a quiet glass of wine. Wine was the drink in Egyptian high society, beer for the masses. Neither ever helped a person struggling with emotions or passions. Wine affects the control centre of your brain. It removes your moral strength just when you need it most! She mulled over Joseph's looks. She imagined; she played in her mind; she tasted, sensed, indulged, perhaps for weeks or months. Nothing satisfied.

Like with the brothers previously, each fantasy weakened her resolve, her good sense, and her better self. She had everything; he had nothing; she could lose everything. But the "longing," like a space launch just before it leaves the ground, consumed everything around it; even learned life lessons were atomized in it. It was now a continuum of discontent that no longer sought pleasure, just a cold end to the pain of burning, hour upon hour of every day. Then one day, she was overcome by surprise, surprised by opportunity!

Imperceptibly, an eye blinks, an empire falters, the natural world groans again. Joseph is back where he came from, just like on that hill at Dothan. But here, human frailty is about to harness the extremes of sinful weakness and secular power in Potiphar's wife to attack a blessing at its human source—Joseph.

She discovers Joseph in the home alone and approaches the slave. But in reality it is a slave who approaches Joseph. While she had idly played with sin in her mind as her unoccupied lazy days passed, Joseph was in a world of hard work. Hard work is a good counteraction to the sins of the flesh. End the day tired mentally and physically, and you will probably be asleep before temptation gets to you! He was also very vulnerable. His life hung in the balance in this foreign land—he was a slave. Surely somewhere during this continual barrage of temptation he remembered the Dinah incident when one sexual sin ended in a whole village being killed by his brothers. Perhaps he feared that the Egyptians would go and kill his family! Fear is also a good deterrent, although somehow we try to convince ourselves in the modern world that it isn't! We also seem to believe that there's nothing to be afraid of in sin. Joseph knew better.

> *But he refused and said to his master's wife, "Look, my master does not know what is with me in the house, and he has committed all that he has to my hand. There is no one greater in this house than I, nor has he kept back anything from me but you, because you are his wife. How then can I do this great wickedness, and sin against God?"*
> —Genesis 39:8–9

The luxury of any kind of personal satisfaction was not open to Joseph at this point in life. So as bluntly and easily as she invited him to sin, Joseph told her why that was a preposterous suggestion. It's likely that she was very beautiful for her position in society. It's likely that she had lots of admirers. It's likely that she usually got what she wanted, with gratitude from the giver. But Joseph refused her! He gave her reasons that were as meditated and studied as her fleshly interests had been. Joseph had been strengthening his moral resolve by daily counting his blessings, while she had been destroyed her moral resolve with indulgence and carelessness. Joseph also believed in God and knew Him. He understood that private matters are not private in any spiritual sense. He had learned this perhaps in the Reuben incident with his father's concubine when a secret got out. God hears. God sees. God knows all about us. Sometimes other people do too.

Being Joseph

So Joseph's final reason for not sinning is the greatest reason: *"How then can I do this great wickedness, and sin against God?"* This personal conviction can keep us from sin. It's a conviction based on a walk in the Spirit in perpetual prayer and worship and gratitude. It's founded on the reading of Scriptures and meditation on them. It's never kept with ease but is always to be fought for and guarded. It's a lifelong commitment to holiness, simply because He is holy. This is what it says: *"Be holy, for I am holy"* (1 Peter 1:16).

"So it was, as she spoke to Joseph day by day, that he did not heed her, to lie with her or to be with her" (Genesis 39:10). Sin is persistent. The one word that raises the ire of hell is "No." The one word that increases the devil's efforts is "No." If you can when tempted, don't talk; just walk away in silence. Temptation is never an opportunity to witness or help people. It's a command to run!

Potiphar's wife spoke to Joseph every day, and every day he said no. Conversation beyond this one word means almost certain defeat in temptation. See Eve in the garden: *"Has God indeed said...?"* (Genesis 3:1). The conversation ends with the fall of man and is followed by all the evil of centuries, following on to Joseph's life and to yours and mine, all from a terrible, tragic failure to say no.

Joseph said no and gave good reasons. And he kept himself busy. Unfortunately, not even keeping busy with work is foolproof.

> *But it happened about this time, when Joseph went into the house to do his work, and none of the men of the house was inside, that she caught him by his garment, saying, "Lie with me." But he left his garment in her hand, and fled and ran outside.*
> —Genesis 39:11–12

This woman was obsessed with this man, who would not give in. She was always on the watch for opportunity, and it came. Nobody was about, and she attacked him with a complete loss of dignity. Like his brothers filled with hate, she was filled with lust. She acted a long way beneath her station in life, insulted her own intelligence (a very weak helper in moral issues), and lunged at him, declaring her complete defeat at the hands of her own lower passions.

This had nothing to do with love or affection, not even simple attraction or beauty. It was rude, basic, and out of control! Do not envy her passion. It's as brutal as the brothers' hatred. Joseph did what the New Testament declares is the right thing to do—he fled (2 Timothy 2:22). Joseph ran away, not dignified, not cool! He escaped—now that's dignified and that's cool! She kept his coat as evidence, yet like his other coat of many colours it declared a lie.

chapter thirty-two

BEING VULNERABLE

And so it was, when she saw that he had left his garment in her hand and fled outside, that she called to the men of her house and spoke to them, saying, "See, he has brought in to us a Hebrew to mock us. He came in to me to lie with me, and I cried out with a loud voice."
—Genesis 39:13–14

The language of Potiphar's wife here is telling. She addresses the men of the house regarding the matter. She claims that Joseph attacked her and left his coat, but she begins her statement with an attack upon Potiphar, her husband! He is to blame, according to what she says. He brought in Joseph, so it's his fault. This small matter could easily be the tip of the iceberg in a bad relationship between Potiphar and his wife. Maybe her mind goes to her husband every time blame needs a hook to hang on. She's inventing the entire fable herself. Her faint conscience is clear enough to tell her that blame is an issue here. She naturally takes it as an opportunity to point to her husband. She may of course have had reason for this. Perhaps there was a disagreement as to buying Joseph in the first place. We don't know.

She doesn't refer to Joseph by name; she calls him *"the Hebrew servant"* (Genesis 39:17). This is all so similar to the brothers and Joseph. They couldn't address him by name until they coined a denigrating one of their own, *"this dreamer."* She also refers to Joseph by his nationality, to insult him, to denigrate him, and to assure all who are listening that he is not one of them! He was and is and always will be a *"Hebrew."*

Further, Joseph is a successful man; many Egyptians were not. Success in a foreign land can work against you, as it has done for many in recent European history. Hard work for the immigrant is okay, but financial success? This is not so easy for locals to accept. It can go dangerously wrong. History has too many examples of foreigners whose only "crime" was being foreign being persecuted, singled out, and like Joseph given a new name, "foreigner."

These are timeless and contemporary realities of human nature, and they are not likely to change until the end of time when sinners from every tribe, tongue, and nation gather around the throne of God to rejoice together as one redeemed people of God (Revelation 7:9). This is why the Word of God has to command us to *"Do not forget to entertain strangers, for by so doing some have unwittingly entertained angels"* (Hebrews 13:2). God's Word acknowledges the difficulty human beings have in integrating. God did a thorough work when He imposed His judgment at Babel! Men have functioned best in clans big and small ever since.

The church is a pilgrim nation, travelling through this alien world. We ought to understand more than most the difficulty of being foreign. We should have a heart for the stranger, and we should go the extra mile in loving and welcoming those who are outcasts. We should see and feel the amazing mercy taught by Jesus in the parable of the good Samaritan, a man who risked his life to help a despised Jew. God help us so to do.

This woman, known to us only as *"Potiphar's wife,"* shows us that there can be a dormant resentment smouldering in individuals and communities against incomers. When the moment is right it can strike with devastation, with innocents being jailed and ruined, and injustice, like in our story, mars a nation's history.

"And it happened, when he heard that I lifted my voice and cried out, that he left his garment with me, and fled and went outside" (Genesis 39:15). The history of men, recorded and unrecorded, is full of the voices of the guilty, crying out against the innocent. *"I*

lifted up my voice," says the guilty woman! Oh that it was the other way around! The guilty speak into the vacuum left by the righteous. The price of freedom of speech unused is freedom of speech misused. Joseph nevertheless did the right thing in running out. From every consideration here, running out was wiser than speaking out!

What are we being told by these incidents involving Joseph's coats? First, he was given a coat by his father because he was his father's special son. The effect of this coat was to provoke jealousy, which being left to fester erupted into hatred. The coat of colours came to represent all that the brothers hated about Joseph.

This is such a reminder of God the Son incarnate. His was a coat of humility, a coat of human flesh, yet as His divinity shone through in acts of miraculous love and mercy, His own people schemed to kill Him. The mob in Jerusalem cried out in the same spirit as Joseph's brothers and Potiphar's wife. They cried out, the guilty against the innocent Son of God, saying, *"Crucify Him!"* (Luke 23:21).

Second, the same coat belonging to Joseph was presented falsely to his father as evidence of his death. At the cross, Jesus' coat was taken from Him, and men gambled for it, a sad reminder of the gamble men take, in every generation, as to whether He's alive or dead. The soldiers gambled. Don't gamble over eternity! Believe the reliable Word of God: Christ is risen!

As Joseph would appear to the brothers soon in glorious royal Egyptian robes, so Christ will soon appear to these soldiers, and indeed to us, in a spotless white robe, *"declared to be the Son of God with power"* (Romans 1:4).

"So she kept his garment with her until his master came home" (Genesis 39:16). What did she think as she held that garment? She certainly had to silence the discomfort of its inarticulate accusation! This fabric coat, its mere material existence, exposed her fabrication of lies. How it condemned her! It made her spine shiver, this coat that she held in her arms. She wrapped it in swaddling cloths of lies and nursed it to sleep. It may have taken her all day, but by the time Potiphar arrived home for supper, she had silenced it and

reshaped it into something not even remotely resembling its sweet innocent origins.

Her lies, made from her most basic animal instinct, self-preservation, condemned Joseph to prison without a trial. This coat, this sightless dumb witness distorted and reshaped for an evil end, proved sufficient material to protect Potiphar's marriage from a smear and sent Joseph to jail.

> *Then she spoke to him with words like these, saying, "The Hebrew servant whom you brought to us came in to me to mock me; so it happened, as I lifted my voice and cried out, that he left his garment with me and fled outside." So it was, when his master heard the words which his wife spoke to him, saying, "Your servant did to me after this manner," that his anger was aroused.*
> —Genesis 39:17–19

Never expect fair judgment from the world, Christian friend. You may not even get a fair trial in the church! But observe the language used here against Joseph. The woman says to the man of the house, "The Hebrew servant whom you brought to us." Is any of this relevant to the issue? No, but none of it is wasted! It's laden with weighty judgments, innuendoes, claims, and blame, none of which can be examined.

Joseph is in Potiphar's family's environment, and there's no chance of a fair hearing and no chance of any examination of facts or claims. Indeed, he is assumed to be guilty before Potiphar even arrives. Such justice is to be expected from ordinary folk, which is why we have lawyers and judges and parliamentary committees and so on. And it's why the old kirk in Scotland had its own courts, to ensure fair hearings for the accused.

See Joseph's Hebrew nationality used against him again: *"the Hebrew."* See his status in society used against him: *"the Hebrew servant."* See the unfair personal implication against her husband: *"The Hebrew servant whom* you *brought to us"* (emphasis added).

This is even an attack upon her own husband. He's to be blamed, as well as Joseph! She called to her aid all the men of the house, as though Joseph had his sights set on hurting them too. She knows there's strength in numbers, even if they are manufactured. She says Joseph *"came…to mock me."* See the self-condemning nature of this statement. Yes, the situation mocked her—she made a fool of herself. She was rejected by a slave. She was seen to be more foolish than a mere slave. So she turns these elements into accusations against Joseph, who is innocent but in a moment found guilty and condemned by a flimsy coat!

SECTION VIII:
BEING IN PRISON

chapter thirty-three

BEING IN PRISON

Then Joseph's master took him and put him into the prison, a place where the king's prisoners were confined. And he was there in the prison. But the LORD was with Joseph and showed him mercy, and He gave him favor in the sight of the keeper of the prison.

—Genesis 39:20–21

Quickly Joseph was put in prison. Note that it was not a normal, common prison but the king's own prison! Joseph then rose to a position of trust and seniority there. What's going on here? How could this all happen so quickly? The Bible says that *"the LORD was with Joseph."*

At this point, Joseph had been accused of attempting to rape Potiphar's wife. He was a slave! He was expendable. In the order of things, Potiphar's wife was much more important, and Potiphar's cursory judgment of the case in favour of his wife was predictable. It shouldn't surprise the reader.

His anger, however, is suspect. How well did he know Joseph? How well did he know his wife? Would it be unreasonable to suggest that he knew both well and that his anger was, in fact, aimed at his wife?

How could he have believed such a story about Joseph? Joseph had evidenced the presence of God in his life. He had been a faithful and diligent servant, and he had gained his master's utmost trust. Until this event, that trust had been well placed. Could it be that Potiphar knew that his wife had an eye for a handsome man?

Potiphar found himself in a predicament. He had to decide quickly how to both deal with a careless wife and protect a faithful servant. He probably saw no choice but to put Joseph in prison. His wife had declared to all and sundry what had happened, so her version of events was now believed as fact by the community gossips.

Potiphar had to deal with it, so he decided that Joseph was expendable. At least this kept his wife quiet in public. The matter was finished, except that perhaps Potiphar used his influence, in the providence of God, to make sure that the keeper of the king's prison understood that Joseph was special and was to be treated well.

This is one way of looking at the text. Why are we told things if not to help us fill in some peripherals? God wanted Joseph to be in touch with the pharaoh, and this would happen in His divine timing.

One might expect a sad story to follow this section, but no. The Lord was with Joseph and showed him mercy. What is there to be sad about if God shows us mercy?

Is this telling us something good about Joseph? Not necessarily. God's blessing is always a result of His abundant mercy. Sometimes our ways please Him. We don't always keep His laws, and we aren't ethically perfect. Our ways can please Him, of course, but we are much more likely to receive God's blessing when we stand up for the gospel, the truth, or God's people.

While grace is God's free and abundant blessing to sinners, saving us from the judgment due for sin, mercy is God's help for sinners who suffer under the consequences of others' sins, and our own sins, in this life. Here Joseph suffered in prison under the consequences of the sin of Potiphar's wife, because of her lies and false accusations against him. But the Lord showed him mercy. What a good God we worship! No wonder Paul and Silas sang in prison!

Please note that the Bible doesn't credit Joseph with winning the favour of the prison warden. Nor does it credit the prison warden with being nice to Joseph. It was God's mercy that affected the warden. The Lord may or may not have used Potiphar. We don't need to know all the details of His secret workings on our behalf. We can just take courage in the fact that God had mercy on Joseph.

So it is with us in life. When things go well for us, we must regard it as God's undeserved mercy. When things go well for our brother, we must praise the Lord for His mercy to our brother, just the same as when the Lord is merciful to us. How difficult it can be for us to *"rejoice with those who rejoice."* Sometimes we find it even harder than to *"weep with those who weep"* (Romans 12:15).

> *And the keeper of the prison committed to Joseph's hand all the prisoners who were in the prison; whatever they did there, it was his doing.*
> —Genesis 39:22

God doesn't always keep us waiting in pain for long periods. So real was Joseph's authority that he was credited with the actions of all those under him. Joseph had a strong influence on those who came into contact with him. May the Lord have such a strong influence on my life as each day passes in the prison of this life.

> *The keeper of the prison did not look into anything that was under Joseph's authority, because the LORD was with him; and whatever he did, the LORD made it prosper.*
> —Genesis 39:23

Here we see God's favour expressed even in such trying circumstances. The prison warden, like Potiphar before him, simply let Joseph do everything he chose to do and didn't get involved. History repeats itself. God would bless Joseph again with favour. Of course we know that this idea is embedded in the name *Joseph*, which means "God will add another blessing." He does and He does and He does! He just keeps adding blessings to His people. What a God He is! Repetition is a theme in the life of Joseph, as will be seen in the rest of the story.

chapter thirty-four

BEING ANGRY

It came to pass after these things that the butler and the baker of the king of Egypt offended their lord, the king of Egypt.

—Genesis 40:1

Here we are about to see Joseph's rise out of the prison into the palace of the pharaoh of all Egypt. Our God, your God, can do such things—for you! So here is how it happened.

It began far away from Joseph. He was not a part of it and knew nothing about it. But God was working on Joseph's behalf in the palace while he was in the prison—maybe like you are? A couple of new inmates arrived. They had offended the pharaoh! And from here, unknown to Joseph or either of them, God was turning things around.

So what were they thinking about, this butler and this baker? Who in their right mind would offend an Egyptian pharaoh? What did they do? Were they part of an insurrection? Did they take some jewels from the palace? Probably not, probably nothing as serious as that. More likely they were targeted because the pharaoh was in a bad mood and took it out on them for reasons we would regard as trivial. But he was the pharaoh, the ultimate ruler, and with the status of divinity. So ordinary men could offend him simply by walking too fast or looking the wrong way or making the simplest of mistakes. The fact that they were put in the same prison as Joseph was, in the house of the captain of the guard, suggests they were regarded not as criminals but more as being out of favour.

Readers who understand what absolute power looks like will turn their minds upward upon reading these texts. People offend God Almighty every day! People today say they don't care! Really? Caution might be counselled for such poor souls. One moment of serious consideration of how much offence has piled up against us and what the wrath of God might look like would caution any wise person against offending such a being. People say they don't "believe" in Him. They say this as though God comes into being because we believe in Him and doesn't exist if we don't believe in Him. What kind of nonsense is this? If merely believing something calls it into existence, then everyone would believe a large bank balance into being! Imagine the baker saying to the butler, "I don't care about Pharaoh because I don't believe in him." Sad, but that's how some people think and speak. The slightest likelihood of God existing should be sufficient for any wise person to realize they should stop doing things that offend Him, just in case He's real!

Surely we ought to realize that believing in something doesn't create it or disintegrate it. Our unbelief is the number-one offence we have committed against Him because we have called Him a liar, brazenly, defiantly, and foolishly!

"And Pharaoh was angry with his two officers, the chief butler and the chief baker" (Genesis 40:2). Pharaoh was angry. Pity them! An angry boss can cause some men to be afraid, but an angry pharaoh, an angry king with absolute power, must be a terrifying thought, let alone sight! This is not hatred, which may remain no more than a bad feeling without practical expression. This anger was the announcement that something bad was about to actually happen!

Anger should be proportionate to the offence, except when an absolute power is angry. There's less restraint because the offence should never have occurred at all to a king! Thus his rage was directed at the butler and the baker, and they were sent to the captain of the guard's house without a trial or a lawyer or a defence. The pharaoh exercised some restraint; he confined them to prison.

"So he put them in custody in the house of the captain of the guard, in the prison, the place where Joseph was confined" (Genesis

40:3). Confinement is a punishment in and of itself. While ancient prisons could be terrible places to live in, they could also be quite civilized and comfortable. Joseph's imprisonment here might be described as civilized. Yet they were still places of confinement.

Confinement was and is still a basic element of punishment in every penal system. Your freedom is taken from you. You are seriously restricted in expression. You can't any longer do what you are capable of doing. Your freedom to live as you are is constricted! You still have all the abilities you had before, but they are all tied up and shut down and contained within these prison walls. So it was for the Son of God to become the man Christ Jesus. His incarnation was an incarceration!

The incarnation of the Son of God is well described as His "humiliation." Here we see confinement at a whole different level. Here we have God confined to human flesh. He who holds the universe in place is Himself held in confinement, by a body of flesh. He can't move outside of this body. And it was the body of an embryo, then a newborn, then a youth. He had to learn to speak, to walk and eat and do everything. He who held the universe in space had to hold His mother's hand! He was the incarnate Son of God. His humiliation was not just the event of the cross, the extreme it was taken to so that we might be redeemed by precious blood. His was a lifelong confinement. Joseph was confined unjustly; Jesus took upon Himself our sins and suffered on our behalf so that we might go free. He bore the anger of God, the Just Judge, for us.

chapter thirty-five

BEING SAD

And the captain of the guard charged Joseph with them, and he served them; so they were in custody for a while. Then the butler and the baker of the king of Egypt, who were confined in the prison, had a dream, both of them, each man's dream in one night and each man's dream with its own interpretation.
—Genesis 40:4–5

Repetition: two men, two dreams, two interpretations.

And Joseph came in to them in the morning and looked at them, and saw that they were sad. So he asked Pharaoh's officers who were with him in the custody of his lord's house, saying, "Why do you look so sad today?"
—Genesis 40:6–7

Joseph's insight is a sign of maturity and experience in reading people. Joseph asks, *"Why do you look sad?"*

Here is one of those ways we communicate without words. Sadly it often goes unnoticed, sometimes even ignored, even by our friends. Please note that these three men are in prison! What made Joseph notice that they were sad on this particular day? Surely they were sad lots of days! Joseph clearly recognized that their sadness this day was due to some new development. What was different in their expressions? How did Joseph know this?

Being Joseph

Verse 4 tells us they were there *"for a while"* before this happened. Joseph had taken time and interest to understand the motions of their hearts, their ups and downs. He recognized that this sadness was different.

My father-in-law, James Russell, was a prisoner of war held captive by the Japanese in Burma for four years in the Second World War. He was with the Argyle and Southern Highlanders, a Scottish regiment. He recounted to me that for these Scottish soldiers, all of their days were sad. Some, like my father-in-law, were in captivity from when they were eighteen years old until they were twenty-two. Some may have been even younger and some a little older, not unlike Joseph in this story. Some were shot and others tortured. There were many beatings. Many died from malnutrition and malaria.

Few survived the "oven." This was a square steel box, like a steel dog kennel, and not much bigger, that men were locked in, just big enough for a small man. There were no windows, and the door was generally a poor fit so a small exchange of air took place, not a lot but extremely hot! They were put in there, often for no reason, sometimes as punishment for some mistake or if they just caught the interest of the guards. Through the heat of the Burmese summer day they would be slowly stifled. They might survive for a day. Unless removed after a few hours they would begin to die, painfully struggling for breath in the extreme temperatures. Exhausted, they were unable to move in the tiny box without being burned against the blistering-hot steel. Their clothes were worn too thin to be of any protection.

Now for them, those were sad days. The whole atmosphere in the camp changed to a heaviness. Men refused to speak at all. They refused their meagre ration of rice to strive in fellowship with their comrade or to die with their comrade. Now that was a sad day! Their looks changed, their conversation ceased, but their determination to stand increased exponentially!

A few survived the oven, even survived being in it more than once. Some would say these were the unlucky ones. The children of these heroes are grateful they didn't give up and die. They lived to tell the tale after the war. They were not asked often, and they didn't talk often. They would be unable to sleep for nights after recounting the memory. They would not talk often about sad days. But like Joseph's fellows, the effect of these sad days on them was noticeable.

They worked, all day, every day, on the Burma railway and the famous, or infamous, bridge over the Mae Kong (depicted as the River Kwai in the movie). Many were permanently maimed physically, and most suffered mentally. Some carried problems for the rest of their lives, and few lived beyond their fifties. The point is that years later, while reluctant to talk about the horrors of war, they still talked about the war years! However, they didn't talk about the sad days. They talked about having fun.

They recounted humorous events and funny moments, lots of them. Many of their happy moments resulted in a beating spree, yet they laughed then as they bled in a fly-infested jungle, and they still laughed decades after. They managed to keep going, even to the point of having fun! Men do overcome, even in the saddest of days. The human spirit can soar like an eagle! Do you? Or is this text for you: *"Why do you look so sad today?"* Lay out your reason and face it and, perhaps, be ashamed!

How is it that the Christian church has become a crutch? Ordinary men can survive the foulest of lives, yet so many professing believers can't last a week. They regard Sunday service as a personal help meeting or a comfort meeting or a pep talk, when it's really a worship meeting, a time to give thanks for the week gone by and to be strengthened by that memory for the week to come. We have fallen so far in faith. Many today come to church looking so sad and like there's nothing new.

For these men in the prison with Joseph, something was new. They had each dreamed a dream.

chapter thirty-six

BEING HUMBLE

And they said to him, "We each have had a dream, and there is no interpreter of it." So Joseph said to them, "Do not interpretations belong to God? Tell them to me, please."
—Genesis 40:8

Before Joseph gives the interpretations of the butler's and baker's dreams, he gives the glory to God. This is humility. Joseph is simply stating the truth. He has no insight or power to read dreams; only God can interpret them. In this statement Joseph isn't trying to impress anyone or make himself important. Many of us say humble words that actually reveal our pride.

Many direct the glory to God simply because they know it's expected of them, but secretly they are quite pleased with themselves. Pride is a subtle sin. It's very good at deceiving even the humble. Humility can't be acted or pretended. Joseph is humble; he's not acting humble. He knows he's really not an interpreter of dreams, but he knows the great interpreter—God. He isn't affected by the fact that they may imagine him to be an interpreter of dreams in some magical way, because he knows he is not. He's not self-deceived. The humility of the truly humble is not an add-on! It's a way of being, like Joseph was at seventeen and all the way through his life. He can say *"Tell them to me"* without it affecting him inside. Humility is an internal way of being. It's nevertheless very clear to the onlooker that it's genuine. If it's not genuine, people realize it instinctively.

> *Then the chief butler told his dream to Joseph, and said to him, "Behold, in my dream a vine was before me, and in the vine were three branches; it was as though it budded, its blossoms shot forth, and its clusters brought forth ripe grapes. Then Pharaoh's cup was in my hand; and I took the grapes and pressed them into Pharaoh's cup, and placed the cup in Pharaoh's hand."*
>
> —Genesis 40:9–11

Imagine, holding the king's cup! So easily said, so easily read, so easily passed over. So profoundly significant.

"The cup of blessing which we bless, is it not the communion of the blood of Christ?" (1 Corinthians 10:16). So says Paul. Yet we restrict it to fifteen minutes a month or three times a year or we go when we feel like it or turn up by accident on Communion Sunday. Brethren, these things ought not so to be!

> *And Joseph said to him, "This is the interpretation of it: The three branches are three days. Now within three days Pharaoh will lift up your head and restore you to your place, and you will put Pharaoh's cup in his hand according to the former manner, when you were his butler."*
>
> —Genesis 40:12–13

Joseph gives the butler the interpretation and then quickly takes the opportunity God had given him to make an appeal to Pharaoh for his release. While the interpretation of the dream is the main point here, we must notice Joseph's comment that so quickly follows:

> *"But remember me when it is well with you, and please show kindness to me; make mention of me to Pharaoh, and get me out of this house. For indeed I was stolen away from the land of the Hebrews; and also I have done nothing here that they should put me into the dungeon."*
>
> —Genesis 50:14–15

His words *"get me out of this house"* reveal an intensity not characteristic of Joseph's speaking. He's normally well-mannered and controlled. Here there's a hint of almost desperation. His normal demeanour is that of contentment. He has learned, like Paul would in a day to come, to be content in whatsoever circumstances he is in (Philippians 4:11). But it doesn't mean that he has forgotten freedom or family. Accepting and being content with the Lord's dealings doesn't require us to give up on legitimate improvements to life.

Joseph says, *"For indeed I was stolen away from the land of the Hebrews; and also I have done nothing here that they should put me into the dungeon."* This is a rare insight into the believer's ability to acquire peace through trusting in the loving purposes of God and the believer's genuine human need for justice among men, the same as any other man needs justice. Joseph's deep inner feeling of being wronged has never left him. It doesn't control him; nor does it govern his every move; but it remains because the injustice remains.

Many are told that they must forgive and forget. This is probably good advice in a real world of real sinners. But in the bigger picture, injustice has an eternal aspect just like sin has. When guilt and no evidence of repentance go hand in hand, there's an ongoing injustice. God will set it right in His wise timing. When He does, we are to rejoice in it, not simply because we have been vindicated but because God has acted like the just judge. That is our God; therefore we rejoice in the Lord when we see Him act as the true God should act. Our rejoicing may appear to look like gloating to the ignorant, but we know that if God takes no pleasure in the death of the wicked, neither will we. We can, however, rejoice in the satisfaction of justice done.

> *When the chief baker saw that the interpretation was good, he said to Joseph, "I also was in my dream, and there were three white baskets on my head. In the uppermost basket were all kinds of baked goods for Pharaoh, and the birds ate them out of the basket on my head." So Joseph answered and said, "This is the interpretation*

of it: The three baskets are three days. Within three days Pharaoh will lift off your head from you and hang you on a tree; and the birds will eat your flesh from you."
—Genesis 40:16–19

How difficult must it have been for Joseph to deliver such a devastating interpretation to the baker! You will die a cruel death in three days! Yet in the exercise of interpreting the dream sent by God, Joseph shows a real understanding of the task. He's not at liberty to pad it out. There's no "political correctness" with the work of being God's spokesman. The old evangelicals regularly pointed out that they were merely postmen. Their work was to deliver God's message without adding to it or taking away from it, with all the passion it came to them with, and to express that accurately. Joseph simply tells it like it is told to him.

Ordinary laymen who were believers also understood their role likewise. They were God's spokesmen in their realm. They also had to deliver God's message without distortion. Today we would argue, with complete confidence, that this is not the way to do it! What has changed? God's Word has not, but we certainly have! Can you imagine a world where believers are not afraid to speak up and be heard, no matter the consequences? Imagine every workplace, every office building, school, shop, sports club, and as many more places as you may add, all of them populated by Christians. Imagine if this week they all began to speak up and tell people the Bible message without fear! That world would be transformed in a few months into a God-fearing society. And all it needs is workplace chatter!

Is it possible that the church can return to such simple roles? Will those unspiritual leaders in our churches, confident yet untaught in the Scriptures, lead in realizing that they have moved the church away from God's Word to a business model or a medical model or a teaching, financial, or entertainment model? Or perhaps saddest of all, a psychological model? None of these models are found in the Bible as patterns for the life of the church! They are ecclesiastically awkward. They don't fit the biblical description of the church.

As has been noted many times, the church is not an organization. It's an organism; it has a life of its own. It's self-perpetuating, and it upholds its members; they don't hold it up! It has its own internal natural order that must be let alone to function. Men want to govern it, and thereby they strangle the life out of it, which is why the church has been reduced to mere buildings and programs and is trussed up by frameworks that look so clumsy, out of place in material and design, on this most beautiful of living organisms. They are grotesque metallic obtrusions sticking out and inhibiting and hurting the body of Christ.

Many of these heresies were learned in secular humanistic universities or in the materialistic world of commerce. God's ways are not learned in classrooms or reading books or attending seminars or doing programs like school children. God's ways are only learned in the furnace of His dealings over years, in prayer, in patient waiting, in learning His Word, in a walk with God. *"Because of his crashings they are beside themselves"* (Job 41:25).

Look at Joseph: he's a man of God. Yet he comes, like so any after him, from the simplest of lives, walking with God in it, trusting Him, believing Him, knowing Him daily, in good and bad times observing His ways in his own heart and also in the lives of others. Joseph tells the baker as he was told, *"Within three days Pharaoh will lift off your head from you."* We can be sure he took no pleasure in this. We can be assured that he didn't soften it or elaborate. He conveyed the message from God as it was given.

What would the church's message look like today if it adopted this principle? But instead of the gospel of God, we have culturally sanitized and detuned the gospel. It's now our own distorted gospel, and it's seen by many with little or no voice to be no gospel at all. If the church of the 21st century would return to the old biblical standards, it would look a lot more like the church in history and like that particular historic church when it stood firm against the world as the alien people of God. Now that church was a profound influence on society! Joseph spoke the interpretations given; so should we.

> *Now it came to pass on the third day, which was Pharaoh's birthday, that he made a feast for all his servants; and he lifted up the head of the chief butler and of the chief baker among his servants. Then he restored the chief butler to his butlership again, and he placed the cup in Pharaoh's hand. But he hanged the chief baker, as Joseph had interpreted to them. Yet the chief butler did not remember Joseph, but forgot him.*
>
> —Genesis 40:20–23

Again, the outcome of the dream is not as important here as the forgetfulness of the chief butler. Ah, the failure of men to remember! How could he forget? Just as readily as we do! Suddenly things begin to go well for him again. Life is good and self is to be pandered to, and the needs of others recede into dark corners of his heart and mind. Joseph is no longer seen as important. Joseph has nothing to give him because he has it all again. Joseph is out of sight, out of mind!

It's easy to be surprised at this man, but we are often not much different. When we first find forgiveness and peace in Jesus we can't help but talk about Him to everyone we meet. A few years pass, and a difficulty or a good partner—or any number of legitimate things—comes along, and we no longer feel the need for forgiveness or peace in Jesus, and we forget.

How often does Scripture tell us to remember the essential things, like *"Remember now your creator"* (Ecclesiastes 12:1) or *"Do this in remembrance of Me"* (Luke 22:19) or *"Remember the Sabbath day"* (Exodus 20:8)? This last text seems to have been totally forgotten in the evangelical churches, squeezed out of mind by materialism and pleasure. The Bible tells us to remember the Lord and His ways often, because we forget often!

The Bible also exhorts us to remember those who helped us in life. Paul says, *"I thank my God upon every remembrance of you, always in every prayer of mine making request for you all with joy, for your fellowship in the gospel from the first day until now"* (Philippians 1:3–5).

To Timothy he says, *"I remember you in my prayers night and day...when I call to remembrance the genuine faith that is in you"* (2 Timothy 1:3–5).

Hebrews presents an encouragement for those who have grown cold. It says,

> *But recall the former days in which, after you were illuminated, you endured a great struggle with sufferings... Therefore do not cast away your confidence, which has great reward. For you have need of endurance, so that after you have done the will of God, you may receive the promise.*
> —Hebrews 10:32–36

None of us got to where we are today without the kind help of others. Don't be like this butler. Be like the Lord, whose Word tells us time and time again, *"He remembers His covenant forever"* (Psalm 105:8).

I hope you know, dear reader, that there are some things that God does forget. He has forgotten the believer's sins! *"I, even I, am He who blots out your transgressions for My own sake; And I will not remember your sins"* (Isaiah 43:25). *"And their sin I will remember no more"* (Jeremiah 31:34).

What is the purpose of the Lord's Table if not to *"do this in remembrance of Me"* (Luke 22:19)? And even among ordinary men the world is speckled with cenotaphs and monuments and statues "Lest we forget."

The butler forgot to remember Joseph, and Joseph remained in the prison. The two words *"this house"* (Genesis 40:14) sum up the period from when Joseph was seventeen until this moment, years of deep personal and spiritual suffering. The Bible seems to emphasize Joseph's anguish when it says, *"Then it came to pass, at the end of two full years"* (Genesis 41:1). Joseph suffered for the most part in silent rest for those two full years, waiting and never losing faith and therefore never losing hope.

God has a purpose in all our misery. Endure it and remember previous days of His blessing. Take encouragement from past blessings until the next blessing arrives, as it surely will!

The great Scottish divine Samuel Rutherford (circa 1600) said in his little book entitled *The Loveliness of Christ*, "Fear not the plough of thy Lord, when it cuts deep furrows in thy back. He is a good husbandman, He purposes a crop!"[6]

---

6 Samuel Rutherford, *The Loveliness of Christ* (Edinburgh: Banner of Truth Trust, 2007).

chapter thirty-seven

BEING RESTORED

Dreams are not confined to adolescents and people in prison. Like spiders, they make their way into kings' houses (Proverbs 30:28). Kings dream dreams too! And even they need an interpreter!

> *Then it came to pass, at the end of two full years, that Pharaoh had a dream... but there was no one who could interpret them for Pharaoh.*
> —Genesis 41:1–8

We are back right in the middle of fantasy again—dreams! This time they carry predictions of events to come. *"Then the chief butler spoke to Pharaoh, saying: 'I remember my faults this day.'"* Notice that he remembers his "faults." True repentance never dresses up its sins. It simply acknowledges the fact without making them worse or better than their true worth. The chief butler tells Pharaoh about Joseph.

> *Then Pharaoh sent and called Joseph, and they brought him quickly out of the dungeon; and he shaved, changed his clothing, and came to Pharaoh.*
> —Genesis 41:14

This is a reminder that when a person is to appear before royalty, a pleasant outward appearance, not just cleanliness, is generally required. It was then, and it is now. The believer who takes care of his or her appearance is not trying to please mere sinful men but showing respect for the Almighty. It's impossible to read the Bible and think God is not concerned about outward appearance. Outward appearance can be a measure of heart appearance even if it can't fool God.

Joseph had a reputation for understanding and interpreting dreams. The believer should have a reputation for understanding how to get right with God, how to be saved from hell, and how to walk with God. He or she should have a reputation for understanding the Bible in its major themes, diligent daily Bible reading, prayer, and attending the gatherings of the church.

Joseph, as was his habit, gave the honour to God but added this wonderful sentence: *"God will give Pharaoh an answer of peace"* (Genesis 41:16). May God give every reader of this book such an answer.

"And Pharaoh said to his servants, 'Can we find such a one as this, a man in whom is the Spirit of God?'" (Genesis 41:38). This is the degree of difference God puts between His people and the worldly man, primarily in spiritual matters, but, as with Joseph, it may be in any area of life God chooses. The youngest believers have the Spirit of God residing in their hearts, and He will give them the words they need to speak when an occasion arises that requires such an intervention. Pharaoh acknowledged that a search is necessary to *"find"* such a one as this. Businesses will tell us that the hardest thing to find is not good products or good markets but good people! Churches likewise often can't find such men, men in whom the Spirit of God dwells. Often they are good men in many other respects, honest, hardworking, experienced, humble, and so on, but spirituality must surely be the greatest search criteria for members, leaders, deacons, elders, and pastors of churches. Numbers in churches mean very little to God or the ordinary man. Even Pharaoh instinctively recognized *"the Spirit of God."* He was surrounded by the best men in all of Egypt, yet a man full of the Holy Spirit was what he needed. And so do we!

"And Pharaoh said to Joseph, 'See, I have set you over all the land of Egypt'" (Genesis 41:41). God can reverse the fortunes of

His children in a moment. Do you believe He can do it for *you*? Pharaoh put Joseph in charge of all Egypt. His interpretation of the dreams was correct. Joseph managed Egypt wisely and was fruitful in that he gathered so much grain as to make him stop counting! He was given a wife and had two sons. As his mother did for him, so he did for his children, giving them names that had real meaning, Manasseh and Ephraim. These two names are wonderful expressions of the goodness of God to Joseph in Egypt.

"Joseph called the name of the firstborn Manasseh: 'For God has made me forget all my toil and all my father's house'" (Genesis 41:51). This statement is a positive reflection of God's goodness in the present, not a miserly gripe about the past. How difficult is it to forget toil and trouble of the kind Joseph is referring to (probably the troubles between Joseph and his brothers)? Many need drugs and counselling. Neither of these have proven to be very reliable. But one blessing from God, and every burden shrinks into insignificance. The past is forgotten in a moment. This is the God of the Bible. He does this all the time for those who trust Him. It's written in the Scriptures all the way through from beginning to end, and it's written in the history of the Christian church for two centuries. Today many testify to this same God overturning their fortunes and troubles and filling their mouths with singing.

One might wonder how Potiphar and his wife felt at this moment. Yet there's no mention of any recrimination towards her. Joseph has forgotten all his *"toil."* God's blessing is such a power for good in the world! Joseph encapsulates all this in the names of his children.

"And the name of the second he called Ephraim: 'For God has caused me to be fruitful in the land of my affliction'" (Genesis 41:52). God does nothing by half. Not only does He deliver us from punishment for sin, He also gives us a robe of the righteousness of His Son and begins a work in us by the indwelling Holy Spirit to *"purify the sons of Levi"* (Malachi 3:3). The gospel delivers us and makes us fruitful where we are. In the land of our affliction, God can make us fruitful. Believe it, look for it, ask for it, expect it!

Being Joseph

Those of us who have experienced such deliverances and blessing can feel Joseph's joy as we read these words. They come alive! Readers feel like they know Joseph; he's a friend and brother. This is the family of God. Readers who understand but have not yet been delivered are filled with the same joy in Joseph's deliverances as they anticipate God stepping into their own circumstances.

> *So when all the land of Egypt was famished, the people cried to Pharaoh for bread. Then Pharaoh said to all the Egyptians, "Go to Joseph; whatever he says to you, do."*
> —Genesis 41:55

People cry out when things get desperate. They may never mention God's name, but even the cry of a child reaches Him in His great mercy. Here a nation cries in hunger to mere men for that which they themselves have no control over—harvests and food. They are in effect praying to their gods, who are mere men, but they know no better here. So God in His great providential care intervenes through Joseph.

In this situation providence is exemplified. We can understand the working of providence in seeing Joseph's organization of Egypt in regards to food. He sees what's going to happen, and he makes provision for it beforehand. Providence is God's foreknowledge and God's provision, just like Joseph here sees the famine, creates storehouses, and delivers the people. This is one of the most dear doctrines of the Scriptures. God is watching over us. We don't know what is happening today, let alone tomorrow! He knows everything, all the time. We have no power to deliver ourselves today, but He has made provision for all of our needs. Why are we, like the disciples in their fishing boat, so *"fearful, O you of little faith?"* (Matthew 8:26).

In John 2 we have a picture of Jesus at a wedding in Cana of Galilee. The host runs out of wine, and Mary tells the servants to go to Jesus and *"Whatever He says to you, do it"* (John 2:5). This is God's recommendation to all the world. Those who are weary with sin, or weary in sin, those without hope, those in bondage, those tired of life, those without God, "Go to Jesus." There, and only there, is hope. The command is also the same: *"Whatever Jesus says to you, do it."* This message has been the same since New Testament times, preached by the apostles and by the church for two centuries, proven to change lives, proven to fill the hungry soul, never a disappointment. The message of the church is to bring men to Jesus. Not to give them hope, but to give them Jesus. Not to give them food, but to give them the bread of life. Not to make them happy, but to implore them to be reconciled to God. Everything that a human being needs is to be found in Jesus Christ, God's own Son.

Joseph fed Egypt and the whole world. Then the food all ran out. Jesus never runs out—there are no lean years, no famines, just joy unspeakable and full of glory to those who believe. Even in a prison cell at midnight they sing; they are a victorious people. No wonder they turned the world upside down.

SECTION IX:
FAMINE

chapter thirty-eight

BEING IN NEED

> *When Jacob saw that there was grain in Egypt, Jacob said to his sons, "Why do you look at one another?"*
> —Genesis 42:1

Joseph's brothers have gone back home. Jacob has mourned; he's still mourning! His life, it seems, is still bound up with the lads. Famine rages in Canaan. He speaks to Joseph's brothers and says to them, *"Why do you look at one another?"*

What's going on? The brothers see that food is diminishing, and they can't see an answer in Canaan. They're sitting at home, quietly looking at each other. Perhaps they each think the other might come up with a solution. Nobody has, but they still sit there, hoping against hope! Jacob sees this silent death creeping on them. They are each waiting on the other to act. But no one knows what to do.

Why is there no record of a conversation with Jacob until now? Perhaps they had no real closeness with Jacob since they returned with the horrific lie that Joseph was killed by a wild beast. Maybe they distanced themselves from him, afraid that too much conversation might lead him to discover their scheme. Perhaps this became the norm. Joseph was seventeen years old when he went to find his brothers. Now he was over thirty. Time can harden attitudes and circumstances, and people just live with them. If you're afraid to talk to God because of what you might have to tell Him, He knows already, yet still invites you to come and reason with Him (Isaiah 1:18)!

Jacob sees the lack of movement, interrupts the lethargy, and says, *"Indeed I have heard that there is grain in Egypt; go down to that place and buy for us there, that we may live and not die"* (Genesis 42:2).

Jacob says, *"The answer is in Egypt; go down to that place and buy for us there!"* How prophetic Jacob is, without knowing it, in sending his sons to Egypt! He's doing what Pharaoh told the Egyptians to do: *"Go to Joseph."* Joseph was the answer. It was a matter of life and death, just as it is for sinners to receive Jesus Christ. Yet some will not come to Him until life has become so unbearable or frightening that they have nowhere else to turn. Unless they are faced with death itself, they refuse to come to Him. When they do come to Jesus they are filled with good things, but they are also filled with disappointment at a life wasted. Many who come to Jesus late in life do amazing things to reach out to friends and family with the gospel, knowing that their end is near. They are impatient to get the opportunity to talk about Him now. They were afraid of losing friends in this life if they became Christians; now they're afraid of losing friends in eternity!

> *So Joseph's ten brothers went down to buy grain in Egypt. But Jacob did not send Joseph's brother Benjamin with his brothers, for he said, "Lest some calamity befall him."*
> —Genesis 42:3–4

The experience of losing Joseph affected Jacob, his father, in his dealings with his other children. Here Jacob is very protective of Benjamin, his youngest. The same thing will not happen again. Jacob is super alert to danger. Many parent are understandably affected like this. They become overbearing and too concerned that trouble might come again. Yet it's unlikely that a tragedy would occur twice in one family. Often the children react against this intensity of care. But Jacob will not let go of Benjamin. Benjamin will not be on hillsides looking after sheep for wild animals to devour. Yet many parents like Jacob, while protecting against imagined evils "out there," miss the danger right beside them. It wasn't wild animals on dark hillsides that hurt Joseph; it was his brothers! And poor Jacob had no clue, then or later, as far as we're told. It's relatively easy to protect from external dangers. The dangers close by are much harder to address, requiring wisdom and clear thinking.

"And the sons of Israel went to buy grain among those who journeyed, for the famine was in the land of Canaan" (Genesis 42:5). This world is in a spiritual famine. God's children are in that world, rising and falling with it in its journeys. They suffer in it and they are blessed in it, but they never find satisfaction or peace until they find Jesus.

God has orchestrated this famine to bring Joseph's brothers to Egypt to meet Joseph again. God is in the famine. God is in the world working out His own wonderful purposes. A great drama is about to be enacted in which they are players, and they have no idea, no clue. They are only thinking about grain to live. But God is going to give them a whole new life. If only they knew, they would be running to Egypt, but they walk heavily. They walk Joseph's route, but there's no fragrance of worship, no balm for sores. They're weary as they walk.

How many a man has gone to church reluctantly, how many a teenager has been dragged to church, and when they find Jesus, they then want to be there every night? "What's this, only one meeting a week?" they say.

God is going to set in motion one of the world's greatest historical events. He will turn them upside down and inside out, but He will finally restore them and restore a whole family. And who are they? They are the very children of Israel!

In their own minds they are nobody special; in fact, they are just another ten sinners. But God had promised Abraham that in his seed all nations of the world would be blessed, and this is all part of that great plan. And God would bring it to pass. Two thousand years ago Jesus came—hallelujah! This is just one of the amazing providences that brought about the birth of Christ the Messiah, the Saviour of sinners. Often those who are nothing are in fact something, and those who seem to be something are, at the end of the day, shown to have been nothing all along! The brothers think they are insignificant among the travellers heading to Egypt. History will remember each one of them by name. Every single one of the brothers' names will be recorded for posterity.

chapter thirty-nine

BEING POWERFUL

Now Joseph was governor over the land; and it was he who sold to all the people of the land. And Joseph's brothers came and bowed down before him with their faces to the earth.

—Genesis 42:6

At this very moment Joseph's first dream comes to fulfillment. His brothers bow before him. It is many years after he naively recounted the dream to them. Time is a component in God's providence that we often find difficult to endure. The brothers don't see this as fulfillment of anything other than a long, hungry, but perhaps hopeful walk! These dejected, mesmerized brothers bow before Joseph, still numb from their long journey, hoping for no more than a few sacks of grain. Ignorant, they are dull in their hearts and minds to all that is happening. The Bible makes the point here by telling us that they bowed *"with their faces to the earth,"* a tired act of homage to—whom? They don't know! They don't care! They can't see; they don't know; they are blind and deaf to what is happening.

As their foreheads touch the ground, the earth feels its curse eased. A whisper of a cosmic breath, slow and peaceful, is heard in the spiritual realm. It's a sigh of satisfaction. A sense of accomplishment is felt in the realm of the Spirit. Another divine plan begins a new chapter. This moment is a milestone, a marker, in a great relentless campaign through time until the Son of God appears. *"Out of Egypt I called My son"* (Hosea 11:1). The poor brothers are only aware of weary muscles and sore feet.

Being Joseph

Joseph saw his brothers and recognized them, but he acted as a stranger to them and spoke roughly to them. Then he said to them, "Where do you come from?" And they said, "From the land of Canaan to buy food." So Joseph recognized his brothers, but they did not recognize him.
—Genesis 42:7–8

This must be one of the saddest moments in the story of Joseph. They did not recognize him. We may excuse them because time had passed and Joseph did act like a stranger, but the situation is profoundly troubling!

So what are we to understand by this *"acted as a stranger"* on the part of Joseph? Does it mean that he pretended to be something he was not? Or does it mean that he truly acted the part of the stranger he actually was? They were strangers in every practical real sense! They were related, but the relationship was thin to say the least, and they didn't even recognize him. There was no working relationship at all there. Joseph's acting as a stranger was the most natural thing in the world towards this set of brothers, even though he recognized them as his "brothers."

Joseph is standing before them, and they don't know it. They are in his presence, and they don't recognize him. Time has changed him, and they have forgotten. The Joseph they sold remains a boy, age seventeen, in their minds, if he's in their minds at all. But Joseph is now a man. He has changed; they have not. They should have grown together, but they have been torn apart. They should have grown closer, but though they look at him intently, seriously, and with fearful concentration, nothing stirs, no question rises, there's no feeling of having seen him before. Joseph is just an Egyptian ruler they have to deal with to get food and then go home.

Joseph fell into a natural stance as a stranger. The fact that we are told he *"acted"* like a stranger means he himself didn't feel like one; why else would he act? He simply acted a part. He wanted to love them and hug them and talk to them and enthuse over them, but how could he with their history? So he acted and went with the flow of events, but how electric were his emotions right then? They were in turmoil. They were sparking and bubbling and churning inside him uncontrollably yet held in place by the uncertainty. Questions and conversations were bursting at the edges of his mind, circulating, appearing, and disappearing, like Jupiter's moons.

So, we might ask ourselves again, how have things developed spiritually in our lives since we were seventeen? How close have you grown to the Lord Jesus? He's still your Saviour, He still knows you, but do you know Him? You have thought of Him as the Saviour of your childhood, but He is the Saviour of your whole life. You may not know Him anymore. He may have become a stranger to you. This is sad, even if common, between brothers, but how tragic between the believer and the Lord Jesus, who died and rose again for us. It's all too common! There are many Christians whose understanding of God has not developed or deepened since they were at children's church. There's little evidence of growth in understanding or in relationship and therefore little growth in experience. It takes only the simplest old gospel hymn to express the question "Are you walking daily by the Saviour's side?" Many of us have not walked daily by the Saviour's side. Too many of us have not heard His voice. We do a religious exercise each morning of reading a daily devotional and saying a little prayer. Little—meaning not short but insignificant! We are still spiritual babies, as Paul says, unable to eat the food of men. Though we are grown, we still need spiritual milk. We haven't developed; we are stunted and weak. This is a common tragic state in many churches today—amazingly, even in whole church groups!

See the brothers before this man, who is in fact their younger brother! They have bowed to the ground in an act of submission. He speaks roughly to them, and they become afraid of him and everything around them. Afraid of what? Well, to them it's Egypt! That's all it is. Joseph is just an Egyptian ruler in Egypt. He's speaking roughly to them, and they are afraid. There's something wrong about them being afraid! They are the sons of Abraham, Isaac, and Jacob. They will be the heads of the twelve tribes of Israel. They will become arguably the greatest nation the world has ever seen, certainly the most significant of all time. Of course they don't know that, but the spirit of the nation ought to be in them even here. How can a nation be born out of fragility?

They are afraid of one man! Not an army or a battlefield; just a granary full of grain. They are so insecure that one man speaking roughly now terrifies them. They took on the entire wrath of the heathen world when they went to the village and killed the man who shamed their sister. Jacob told them that they had aroused the wrath of all the great nations of that country. They were unafraid and defiant. *"Should he treat our sister like a harlot?"* (Genesis 34:31). Now that's fighting, winning, talk!

The brothers have changed. They have shrivelled up inside with the problems of life. Their nagging consciences have tired them. Their fears and recriminations have exhausted them. Sin has weakened them, and they have no fight left in them, so much so that a simple but serious question roughly put leaves them shaking and frightened to silence.

Many a believer is afraid of serious conversations, even serious conversations about God, about our heavenly Father! They are frightened of serious spiritual matters. This is the brothers as Joseph speaks roughly to them. *"Where do you come from?"* (Genesis 42:7). This potentially innocent question is heard as hostile by its tone, and they are afraid. The question is innocent. All they are afraid of is a strong tone!

How can it be that their younger brother whom they used to bully is now making them afraid? It's so because they have not grown, not developed, but remained where they were. Note that unconfessed serious sins stunt the growth of God's people. Unresolved serious issues in relationships leave God's people stuck in a spiritual time warp. A lack of daily walking with God in the light of His Word leaves many believers immature and frightened of everyone and anyone who speaks wrongly to them. They need to be nursed and protected. They are cautious of anyone who is confident, even confident in the things of God.

Joseph has grown by the exercise of trust, by walking in faith. In life's hardships and trials and the temptations he resisted, he stood the test of time and has become a man of God while his brothers are stunted and small. Yet we know they are, in fact, this incredibly powerful Egyptian ruler's family—his brothers!

> *Then Joseph remembered the dreams which he had dreamed about them, and said to them, "You are spies! You have come to see the nakedness of the land!"*
> —Genesis 42:9

It seems that Joseph's memory of his dreams provokes an instant critical, even interrogating, response! Where is the love, the forgiveness, the acceptance, the open unquestioning welcome for sinners? What's happening here? Has Joseph lost his self-control? Surely not—but maybe? Is Joseph being clever, as some say? Perhaps. Is he merely checking up to make sure that this father and his brother Benjamin are in good standing, as others suggest? Is he simply asking some test questions to see if they have changed before he shows them his true self in unconditional love? Perhaps.

We read, desperately superimposing our 21st century Christian cultural psychology on poor Joseph. Can we allow him to speak for himself? Can we read without our distorted lenses on? Can we hear the Bible and let it contradict us, challenge us? Or are we like these brothers, too insecure to be challenged, even by God?

We struggle and strive because we must show him to be super warm and fuzzy, to the point of absolute unreality. But we don't really know any real people like this fuzzy believer we have forced on the Christian image as though it resembled the Lord Jesus Christ. Jesus Christ was a strong man, unafraid of conflict, even though He didn't enjoy it. The true believer in the Bible is not at all warm and fuzzy, and neither is Joseph right now!

It's easier to see this outburst as the first visible crack before the disintegration of a great emotional dam, even in this beautiful man called Joseph. He attacks them from his position of absolute power: *"You are spies!"* That is a death sentence! Joseph is acting justifiably as the stranger that he is to them. They didn't want him as a brother. Now he will show them what that means for a while. Is this deliberate evil on Joseph's part? No! Is it sinful unforgiveness or unloving revenge? No, absolutely not! Joseph is totally within the bounds of reasonable reactions upon seeing these men. They would have killed him! They sent him into slavery to let someone else kill him. They sold him to foreigners and strangers and devastated his beloved father by telling him that his son was dead. What had they done to Benjamin? These men deserve no mercy from Joseph. They haven't done anything, or said anything, that requires any good response from Joseph at all. Joseph is restraining himself but is set to explode if necessary. He's also releasing some water from that emotional dam to let them sense the level of emotion that awaits them.

There must be something different here from his last meeting with them, at the hill of Dothan. Because this "dreamer" has just awakened! His latent indignation is legitimate and limitless, awesome, and righteous. The dam will burst very soon, releasing energy pent up for years. Grace is able to defuse righteous indignation! Joseph's indignation is righteous. At this moment Joseph doesn't know if the dam inside will release grace or judgment. He clearly hopes to find some vestige of change in his brothers to release mercy.

The discomfort the brothers feel is their conscience striking a chord with Joseph's legitimate antagonism. The whole event is like a massive lake of pain slowly pressing against a dam that's been weakened by the relentless passage of time. Their meeting is the last straw; it will soon disintegrate!

Through the years until now Joseph had left it all behind him. Day by day he functioned; he lived and laughed and did a good job. The consequences of these men's hatred remained unchanged. Joseph was not guilty of harbouring grievances. But he had broken bones that had not been healed. Nobody had *"healed the hurt of My people"* (Jeremiah 6:14). Joseph had been left to suffer to this very day before us in the text.

Joseph is a man who carries what we superficially call "baggage." He's understandably affected deep inside, and permanently so. He has just realized the whole story from dream to reality! It has been a long time in coming, this day. A long time since he was young, being seventeen.

These brothers are actually now as naive as Joseph was at seventeen! They have no inkling of the rage they could have aroused, the level of emotional turmoil they have raised. They, like Joseph all those years before, have no idea of the size of the problem they are facing.

If only we could have warned Joseph back then about the brothers' corporate rage. If only we could have called out, "Joseph, your life is in danger!" Why did his father, Jacob, not tell him about his own experience offending his older brother? Why did he send Joseph to his brothers in the first place? Joseph had no clue back then, at seventeen. To him it was just a dream! The brothers here are just as bewildered after all. They just want a bag of grain!

Sometimes our expectations of those who have been hurt badly are cruelly unrealistic, even downright wrong. We have not yet been shown clearly what was going on inside Joseph. We can interpret freely within the boundaries of biblical sense, but before we leave it and move on to a clearer moment, let's try to stand in Joseph's shoes before we conclude that this is all a cool, calculated drama—just an act!

Here we are told that he remembered the dream. He had not carried this dream with him every day of his life. He forgot it for long periods. It was no longer at the forefront of his mind. The pain was seldom far away from his heart. He went to bed at night a foreigner in a foreign land. But here, faced with his brothers bowed to the ground before him, the memory of his dreams startled him. He remembered!

It would be understandable for Joseph to be deeply upset with these ten men. We need not recount their sins. We can feel the resultant pain in the conversation.

Can we allow Joseph to be upset, even vindictive? Can the present-day church find an ounce of an excuse for Joseph? Can Joseph vent? We can't! It's not allowed today in the church. There's no possibility to speak your pain like the psalmist did. Like Jesus did! Like Paul did, like the historical church did, without caution. "Sticks and stones may break my bones, but names will never hurt me" says the childish rhyme. But we have grown so soft that mere words bruise us easily. Sometimes the only ease for the hurting person is to be able to use words freely. Angry words, pain-filled words, words saturated by anguish! Words, words, words—they are only words! No one will die because of them like Joseph might have at the hands of these men before him. There must be a time for hurting people to grieve and nurse their wounds with all the words at their disposal.

If Joseph is to be treated like many church members today who have been hurt, then he must not express any Psalm-like words. Nor will he be given time to heal. Unconditional and instant forgiveness is the unreal standard of the modern church. There can be no recriminations, no reserve, no reminders, no consideration for the pain of years. The loss in human dignity and familial relationships, the sheer agony of Egypt—all must be laid aside, instantly. No memory can cloud the believer's mind. No scar is to be seen. There are no exceptions to the rule, just self-giving love and forgiveness. It's as though the modern church has never read the Psalms of David or heard the outcries of Jesus against the Pharisees!

Joseph, unchained by modern hypocrisy, is going to put these brethren through a time of emotional strain. He has had to endure it for half of his still young life. Judge him carefully, because *"With what judgment you judge, you will be judged"* (Matthew 7:2).

"But he said to them, 'No, but you have come to see the nakedness of the land'" (Genesis 42:12). It's very likely that Joseph never expected to see his brothers ever again. He's caught off guard, and he simply responds as he feels. He seeks to ensure that they are his brothers; he pushes them by accusation; he puts them back on their heels, disconcerts them. Seeing their weak response, he naturally proceeds with his line of questioning. Does he enjoy their discomfort? No, probably not. Is he indulging in recriminations? No, he's being quite normal. He's expressing his pain in a cautious way. It isn't contrived or prepared speech. This is the language of pain.

Being Powerful

We would love to twist it and demand that it be seen as the language of innocent cleverness. However it's very reasonable to consider that we are seeing Joseph's pain expressed where it rightly belongs, and spontaneously. The fact that he is interrogating them is just the way it comes out. This is not the language of rage or hate, just the natural bursting of a dam that has been held in place by circumstances beyond his control for years. He slowly, as he speaks, brings it into control and becomes deliberate. Now the attitude that naturally erupted from the "stranger" has been adopted, and he is going to run with it, consciously acting the part, but with purpose, which is not yet clear to the brothers or even perhaps to Joseph. Of course we know where it will end. Joseph acts as though he is interrogating them. He pushes them away. They don't know how to react, and they're afraid of him. He's a threat to them.

The superficial Christian, the weak believer, the believer who has not fed his soul on the deep things of God, is a spiritual child. The Christian man who has remained in the shadows of God's church is immature and weak. He may have taught in Sunday school or served as a deacon and been a busy person in the externals of the church, but he's not a spiritual man. He may have been a church treasurer or played in the worship team. These are the fringes of Christianity. They don't produce growth in a believer. They leave the physically grown man a mere child in spiritual terms.

Prayer, serious Bible study, and the application of truth to daily life are the essentials of spirituality. A walk of faith and God's breakings and dealings, as in the life of Joseph, are what change us. These make us grow deep in the things of God. These experiences make us strong and cause us to grow into full-grown men and women of God. The churches of today have moved away from the real essence of the biblical Christian life. They have replaced identification with Christ in His sufferings with mere superficial identification with a church culture. They have sent God away, sold Him into a slavery to their own ideas. Thus they have remained little people when they should be full-grown people of God.

Joseph's brothers were afraid because of lack of a walk with Joseph's God. Had they even walked in the footsteps of their father in his younger days, they would never have been broken men like they appear to be now. The man of God is not afraid of anything other than God Himself! No man terrifies God's people. They have stood daily in the presence of His almighty power as they prayed and beseeched Him who is the God of all the earth to move in power in the salvation of souls. No man can make them cringe with fear. Their boldness, as the New Testament shows, is a characteristic that shakes the confidence of their oppressors. Kings with the power of life and death actually fear them!

The weakness of the brothers is a sign of backsliding. However, There's also an added element of humility. This is clearly a different set of men from those who planned and executed the sale of their brother Joseph into slavery. These men have had time to help their recovery and time to work on self-examination. It has left them weak and disheartened, fragile and afraid. It has worked in a humility, the humility that comes from a better knowledge of self. However, because they didn't use that time to put things right, they are only halfway to healing.

Humility produced by failure is not what God wants. God wants those who have seen their own sins and failures, their corruption, to then look to Him and find cleansing by the blood of Christ and fresh filling with God's Spirit and thereby a new life from above. This meeting with God Himself, this dealing with God in real experiential terms, is necessary to restore them to a spiritual equilibrium. Then their humility is made a strength by being balanced with forgiveness, cleansing, and acceptance as they are brought into the close family of God, accepted in the beloved!

God gave the brothers that time. The Lord waited for them. They didn't come to Him. So slowly they grew silent, and fear became their "being."

Time itself sometimes pushes real self-examination into men's and women's hearts. When they grow old they say things that seem out of character. They become softer, more easy to live with, more open to excuse or see the other's point of view, less likely to insist upon their own opinions. It can be just the fatigue of aging. It can also be the work of the Holy Spirit. The brothers reveal a humility and softness that, though they are weak, are the beginning of strength. Spiritual, or at least moral, strength. The conversation deepens.

chapter forty

BEING TWELVE BROTHERS

And they said, "Your servants are twelve brothers, the sons of one man in the land of Canaan; and in fact, the youngest is with our father today, and one is no more."
—Genesis 42:13

"*Your servants*": they were free men in Canaan until the famine. Hunger makes a man a servant. Poverty is dangerous. Hungry people are vulnerable to evil causes.

Consider the content of this brief confession of who they are. "*Your servants are twelve brothers.*" This must be seen as a development from earlier days. Soon after Joseph was removed, there was a case for seeing them split up and separated. Here they have clearly come together and are willing to describe themselves as "*twelve brothers.*" There's something harmonic about the phrase. Something together and strong. Twelve brothers. Yet they appear so weak. Why? Could it be because "*one is no more*"? There are twelve notes in the chromatic scale. Imagine the music that would be lost if just one of the twelve notes in the chromatic scale went missing! No F sharp or no B flat. Perhaps no G for J. S. Bach to write "Air on the G String." So many wonderful musical moments would never have been possible, and that in every musical genre.

The brothers were notably incomplete. But they were prepared to acknowledge that they were "*twelve brothers*"; it's almost poetic!

All these years, all the hatred. Yet still the absent one occupied a place in the twelve.

It's not easy to get someone who has been a part of your life out of your life! The bereaved tell us this; the divorced tell us the exact same thing. Parents tell us this. We know this ourselves, but still we try, like the brothers did, to get rid of the problem by separation, to one degree or another. Sometimes the one who is "no more" is more present than those who are always with us. A philosopher, Jean Paul Sartre, talks of going to meet a friend in a busy café, and when he arrives, his friend is not there; his seat is empty. At that moment he's more conscious of the absent person than of all the people present!

So, at times, are the brothers more conscious of Joseph than of all the people around them, because they can't expunge him from their consciences! They are weakened by the loss of their brother, although they perhaps don't realize it.

"But Joseph said to them, 'It is as I spoke to you, saying, "You are spies!"'" (Genesis 42:14). In other words, Joseph calls them enemies, foreigners with an evil purpose. *"You are among us, but you work for another state that is opposed to us."* They are not *"servants,"* Joseph says. They are enemies, spies! To establish this as true or false, they will be tested.

Here is Joseph turning in his spirit. He sees an opportunity to find out about Benjamin. *"In this manner you shall be tested: By the life of Pharaoh, you shall not leave this place unless your youngest brother comes here"* (Genesis 42:15). Is it possible that the mere mention of Benjamin touches a warmer note deep inside him? Is there more going on inside Joseph than is going on inside the brothers? There could very well be!

They are to be tested by bringing their youngest brother back with them. If they can show a genuine relationship with Benjamin, then they are not spies, not enemies, but family. Not just friends or colleagues or fellow workers—they are full-blown family.

God sees like this on a Sunday morning. He says to many in the quiet of their hearts as they seek to approach Him, "Where is your brother? Where is your sister? You can't come here without them! You will receive no food here until they are with you!" But week in, week out, in churches all over the world, there are empty seats that mark us out as suspect. The one judging us is looking for the absent brother. The brother pushed away; the brother offended, hurt, rejected; the brother disillusioned, discouraged, who gave up. Yes, he still is being looked after by his heavenly Father. But he should be looked after by us as well.

Such a sorry but accurate picture of many churches today! We are broken and divided and separated and all messed up. Often we know what the problem is but refuse to fix it. We blindly carry on in life without the brother who is not with us, imagining that God is as unmoved by his pain as we are. He gave His Son for that brother. Joseph didn't give up on seeing Benjamin. Neither should we give up on fixing divisions with people who once walked with us in the things of God but left.

There's a story in the gospels about one sheep in a flock of one hundred—you know the story. It was out on the hills far off from home—you know the sheep. Take it to heart; go and find the sheep and bring him or her home to the family of God this Sunday.

The evidence Joseph wants to see is Benjamin with his other brothers. He wants to see them all together. He can rightly doubt the truth of their protestations if they can't bring Benjamin.

> *"Send one of you, and let him bring your brother; and you shall be kept in prison, that your words may be tested to see whether there is any truth in you; or else, by the life of Pharaoh, surely you are spies!"*
>
> —Genesis 42:16

Joseph says if they don't bring their brother, that's sufficient evidence that aren't what they say they are. What if Benjamin refuses to come? Maybe the Lord will change his attitude before they even get back to him!

"So he put them all together in prison three days" (Genesis 42:17). He puts them *"all together"* in the prison. Sometimes things have to get worse before they get better. It would seem that the brothers need to be pressed together more to bring them to the place

of full repentance. Three days in prison is a lot of time when you're under pressure. The mere mention of Benjamin coming down to Egypt is sufficient to take them back in time to Joseph going down to Egypt. God has wonderful ways to gently, or harshly if necessary, bring us to the place where we face up to things in spiritual terms.

"Then Joseph said to them the third day, 'Do this and live, for I fear God'" (Genesis 42:18). Oh that God would give us rulers who fear Him! Joseph's tone has changed. Perhaps thoughts of a family reunion are getting stronger; perhaps his hurts are taking a second place to seeing Benjamin. He has moved from his original demand that one brother go back to Canaan to get Benjamin while the other nine stay in prison. Now he says one brother will go to prison, and the other nine can go to get Benjamin. He presents this suggestion as though having moved to a more friendly mindset.

Joseph speaks to them on the *"third day."* The elements of this text are full of pointers to the Lord Jesus Christ at the resurrection. *"Do this and live."* Joseph says he fears God in a way that suggests a belief similar to that expressed by the centurion at the cross: *"Truly this was the Son of God!"* (Matthew 27:54). We are not given a complete picture as to the individual's belief, only a cautious statement to give us hope. Joseph gives them hope by this reference to God: *"for I fear God."*

"If you are honest men, let one of your brothers be confined to your prison house; but you, go and carry grain for the famine of your houses" (Genesis 42:19). Now he's thinking of them taking grain to their "houses"; this is without doubt a genuine softening. Things, it seems, are beginning to change. That is, Joseph is changing. He is softening.

"And bring your youngest brother to me; so your words will be verified, and you shall not die" (Genesis 42:20). *"So your words will be verified."* *Words* and *die* are used in the same sentence. Words are serious. Jesus is the Word of God incarnate. God spoke a word, and the heavens were created; He *"breathed into his nostrils the breath of life; and man became a living being"* (Genesis 2:7). The ten commandments were spoken to Moses. They are called the Ten Words.

The gospel, the Good News—words—was preached by Jesus, and the church was commanded to go and preach the gospel. The gospel is a "word." Jesus spoke a word, and they were healed. Here Joseph's brothers have one of life's reversals on their hands. They had lied to Jacob and not brought Joseph back. Now they must tell the truth, and the evidence of their truthfulness will be Benjamin coming back with them to Egypt. It's a reversal of the situation with Joseph, but they feel the similarity, the connection of events, enough to turn their minds to recriminations over Joseph among themselves. They think they can speak without Joseph understanding them. Language has been used for and against mankind since Babel. The brothers think their language is hiding their conversation from Joseph, but it's the other way around! In fact it's Joseph who is hiding the fact that he understands perfectly everything they are saying.

When we come before God our words have to be verified. Never think that you can say what you like in the presence of God without consequences. He tries words. He examines us. This is why Ecclesiastes says, *"When you go to the house of God...let your words be few"* (Ecclesiastes 5:1–3). These are good words.

chapter forty-one

BEING GUILTY

> *Then they said to one another, "We are truly guilty concerning our brother, for we saw the anguish of his soul when he pleaded with us, and we would not hear; therefore this distress has come upon us."*
> —Genesis 42:21

See the depth of the work that it takes to bring men to the place where they say, *"We are truly guilty."*

How many words flow freely from our mouths hour by hour—so smoothly, with no resistance, they just glide off our tongues. Effortless! But the word *guilty*—what a monumental effort is required to say it. Have you ever admitted before God that you are guilty? Then note this: you were only able to say it because He gave you grace to do so! It is not in the human heart to admit guilt. Hear our father Adam's confession. Maybe he meant to say *"guilty"* but couldn't get it out. He only managed to say, *"The woman whom You gave to be with me, she gave me of the tree, and I ate"* (Genesis 3:12). Now that's the truth about us—we're only really able to say that someone else is guilty!

Are we to understand that this is the first time the brothers have discussed the subject? Maybe! Maybe not! But this is the first time they have understood their guilt, the first time that guilt has invaded their hearts and minds, filling them with a fearful expectation of judgment. This is gospel repentance being worked into their hearts. Have you felt it?

And Reuben answered them, saying, "Did I not speak to you, saying, 'Do not sin against the boy'; and you would not listen? Therefore behold, his blood is now required of us."

—Genesis 42:22

Reuben says, *"Did I not speak to you…?"* God is never without a witness. He has His servants in every situation where they are required. Reuben told them, and in effect they didn't listen, because Joseph became as good as dead to them. But the warning was given. God was trying to keep them from sinning against Joseph; He was giving them a way out. When temptation comes, watch for that way. And remember, there's always a way out. You may have to look for it, but it's always there.

Here Rueben is not blaming the others, because he knows he was complicit by his absence. He knew they were planning and discussing it, so why was he not there? Did he leave to avoid the decision? Was he afraid to stand up to them? We don't know what went on in his mind. He includes himself in the guilt: *"His blood is now required of us."* This suggests that he does see his own part in the whole event.

"Therefore behold" (Genesis 42:22). Ah! They're finally connecting the dots of life and seeing themselves as part of something. They thought they had made a discovery of note. They had! But only a fraction of the truth had dawned upon them.

Joseph was listening to all of their conversation. He saw a genuine change, a real sorrow for what they had done, not just a discomfort with their present circumstances. Often men repent because of trouble. It's said that there are no atheists on a fishing boat in a storm, but they all reappear in the calm of the harbour. That is not true repentance. True repentance declares itself with no consideration of benefits. True repentance is interested in honesty, in truth. *"Depart from me, for I am a sinful man, O Lord!"* (Luke 5:8). This is true repentance! Those who truly repent might seek mercy, but they will seek it with the certain knowledge that in no way is it deserved.

Another real evidence of true repentance is that it produces tears, tears in the individual repenting and in the one the repentance is aimed at. Here, Joseph turns away.

"But they did not know that Joseph understood them, for he spoke to them through an interpreter" (Genesis 42:23). Many people think that God doesn't know what they're saying and doesn't listen, and even if He did, He would not understand. He does. He speaks your language and understands your emotions, your way of thinking, your heart, and your head. He understands you as you are, intimately. He doesn't need an interpreter or any other go-,between, a priest or a minister. You can go directly to Him, confident of getting answers that are true and will work.

You do have an advocate with the Father. An advocate defends us before a judge. The Bible says that our advocate is Jesus Christ the righteous (1 John 2:1)! Can we emphasize this point too much? No! Hear it again: God knows you personally, everything about you. He loves you, and He wants to meet you and talk and walk and fellowship with you, but you need to be reconciled to Him. You need to be made right in your relationship with Him through believing in Jesus Christ. Do you believe? God wants to talk to you about this.

"And he turned himself away from them and wept" (Genesis 42:24). Joseph could have left matters here. He could have put them all to death as spies right away and got on with his comfortable, successful life in Egypt, having a satisfying sense of vindication. Why was he weeping?

"Then he returned to them again, and talked with them" (Genesis 42:24). Up until this text in this part of the story the Bible tells us that Joseph spoke "to" the brothers. Here for the first time, the Bible says Joseph talked *"with them."* Here is a real softening, and they don't see it.

They have no idea how close to the edge they have come. They see Joseph turn away, but they have no idea what he is thinking. He turns to them, and as the angelic host breathe a sigh of relief, the brothers hold their breath! The angels again smile to one another while the brothers exchange glances of helplessness, for fear of what is next. Joseph has turned to them again, after turning away!

Maybe you feel like God has turned away from you. Maybe you failed, and you let go of any sense of His presence, or you gave up, thinking He had gone away. God may turn away, but He will not go away. He may let you think He has gone away for a while to chasten you, but He is just at the door. He will turn back again if you seek Him with all you heart, soul, mind, and strength.

Joseph returned to his brothers and talked to them. *"And he took Simeon from them and bound him before their eyes"* (Genesis 42:24). This "binding of Simeon" was not for Joseph's sake, of course. Did Joseph have him treated as roughly as his brothers had treated him? Perhaps the big question is how they felt when they saw Simeon bound roughly before them. Did it bring fear of what this Egyptian ruler could do to them? Hopefully some little glimmer of a memory stirred, forcing their thoughts back to the Dothan pastures. Did they feel in themselves the uncomfortable memory of Joseph's striving to get free? God has ways of taking us back in time to make us feel today what we should have felt long ago! If they did, it would be a sign of an encouraging softening. Such a softening is without doubt evident to Bible readers as they read the story but wasn't so evident to Joseph yet.

Joseph could have fed on bitter thoughts and nurtured a just case against his brethren through the years, but he didn't. He could have rehearsed what he would do or say to them, like they rehearsed their hateful schemes against him. We all when unjustly treated go through this process of reliving in our minds the details of the injustice, listening to the backwards screeching of jumbled conversations as they rewind and play again in our heads. All sorts of bad attitudes are fostered when we allow ourselves this freedom.

Joseph has none of that anger. He shows nothing but legitimate pain, which is here quickly developing into a search for truth and an apparent growing interest in his brothers. It's hard to see anything other than a real man travelling through pain to forgiveness. There's no trace of bitterness and no sign of revenge, no need for going over too much of the past, just enough to learn the lessons and then move on to richer fellowship.

Many people struggle with these kinds of situations, and some never overcome them. Hebrews 12:14–15 says, *"Pursue peace with all people...looking carefully lest anyone fall short of the grace of God; lest any root of bitterness springing up cause trouble, and by this many become defiled."* The seeds of bitterness spring up suddenly; they also die relatively quickly. But if fed for a long enough time bitterness becomes part of the person, like when a vine strangles a tree. It becomes difficult to separate the two without causing serious damage to the tree itself, and if allowed to grow without restraint, the vine will kill the tree completely. Consider this also: bitterness in one results in defilement of many! What a warning!

Bitterness is not evident in Joseph. He is a worthy child of a good God. But pain has shown its colour through these dealings with his brothers. Look here at the grace and godliness of this man in his restraint when faced with cruel enemies. This is the grace of the believer. There are few reasons for forgiveness more powerful than the Christian message, mirrored here profoundly in this Old Testament saint.

> *Then Joseph gave a command to fill their sacks with grain, to restore every man's money to his sack, and to give them provisions for the journey. Thus he did for them.*
> —Genesis 42:25

Surely the Scripture says *"Thus he did for them"* with an air of amazement. They still don't know who he is!

Here things begin to get a bit complicated. But it's easy to see in this a picture of the love of God for His children travelling through this foreign land to our home. He fills our sacks; He gives back all we have given. He makes provision for us. One of the most beautiful doctrines in the Bible is the doctrine of God's providence. He sees in advance and makes sufficient provision for every event. Every moment, we are provided for. Hence the New Testament asks with an amazed confidence, *"He who did not spare His own Son, but delivered Him up for us all, How shall He not with Him also freely give us all things?"* (Romans 8:32).

"So they loaded their donkeys with the grain and departed from there" (Genesis 42:26). Can you feel their relief? Do you feel for their ignorance! Even with Simeon's imprisonment, oh, the open road to Canaan! The road they trod with heavy hearts now spells freedom!

"But as one of them opened his sack to give his donkey feed at the encampment, he saw his money; and there it was, in the mouth of his sack" (Genesis 42:27). Could it have been twenty shekels of silver?

The Bible doesn't give the name of this brother. We might read too much into it if it did. They are all in this together as one man in this story. Only this one discovered his money in his sack at the encampment; the others discovered their money in their sacks when they were at home with their father, Jacob.

> *So he said to his brothers, "My money has been restored, and there it is, in my sack!" Then their hearts failed them and they were afraid, saying to one another, "What is this that God has done to us?".*
>
> —Genesis 42:28

They said, *"this that God has done to us,"* thinking that God was punishing them for their sins, when all the while God was preparing a blessing! Note how the natural man connects bad occurrences with his own sin and a God he sees as a judge. At least they show that God is not far from their thoughts and is getting closer by the day.

chapter forty-two

BEING HONEST

Then they went to Jacob their father in the land of Canaan and told him all that had happened to them, saying: "The man who is lord of the land spoke roughly to us, and took us for spies of the country."
—Genesis 42:29–30

This journey, so profound for Joseph so long before, so recently sad for the brothers, is not passed over so quickly as they go home.

It seems like they are telling Jacob everything that happens now. No more secrets, no more lies. No more hiding. But they are still blind and may not even understand how to fix themselves. Just like us!

"But we said to him, 'We are honest men; we are not spies'" (Genesis 42:31). Sinners can be amazingly bold when accused of something they did not do. They often make claims that are not true to support the one little true moment. They are not spies. Neither are they honest. They have been living a lie since they sold Joseph. Here is evidence to encourage us: they tell the truth; they begin to resemble honest men.

"'We are twelve brothers, sons of our father; one is no more, and the youngest is with our father this day in the land of Canaan.' Then the man, the lord of the country, said to us, 'By this I will know that you are honest men:

Being Joseph

Leave one of your brothers here with me, take food for the famine of your households, and be gone.'"
—Genesis 42:32–33

Joseph challenged their honesty. He knew this was the weak point in their protestations. Truth is a much bigger concept than mere honesty in speech. Their talk among themselves that he overheard seemed to show a change in his brothers. Joseph wanted to know how thorough any change was. It was not sufficient to merely present a verbal claim; it had to be verified by practical evidence.

So it is with the gospel and the claim that "I have become a Christian." The words are easy; the lifestyle demands that we carry a cross and give up our lives to Him. Many of us fail to show a visible allegiance to Jesus and His call to carry the cross. But there's lots of evidence that we are committed to church culture. This is not at all convincing, because church culture has innumerable benefits in friendships and help and support and good teaching. There's no cross these days in holding to a church culture in the Western world. That is undoubtedly changing, and the reality of present-day professions may be challenged. Make sure you have lived the life.

In giving them food for their households, Joseph was making a concession to them. These were cracks in the dam of emotional pain as well as his strong challenges. Joseph didn't know what he was dealing with yet. As the brothers recounted the happenings to Jacob, we can't imagine the pain he felt as he heard the demand to bring Benjamin to Egypt!

> *"And bring your youngest brother to me; so I shall know that you are not spies, but that you are honest men. I will grant your brother to you, and you may trade in the land.'" Then it happened as they emptied their sacks, that surprisingly each man's bundle of money was in his sack; and when they and their father saw the bundles of money, they were afraid.*
> —Genesis 42:34–35

What are we to understand by this strange gesture of the money in the sacks? Is Joseph breaking down in his hurt and desperately trying to show affection in surprising ways? Is he trying to test them or playing with them? Is he toying with the fact that they sold him into slavery? Each man's money was restored. Why did they pay individually when they travelled as a family group? Are we making things too complicated? Is it a simple kindness? We will never know for certain until eternity.

Whatever the intention in Joseph's heart, the brothers are bewildered to the point of fear. They are afraid, and Jacob is afraid! They're afraid at the sight of "bundles of money." They are as confused as we might be as to the precise meaning of these bundles. For many people in every society that ever was, the bundles would actually be a great cause for rejoicing. Yet they are afraid! Can it be that the Bible is showing us two different sources that produce fear, to compare the brothers' fear and Jacob's fear?

The brothers' fear is not simply of this strange Egyptian ruler. Nor is it the fear that they are going to die. They are afraid of the Egyptian ruler, and they understand that it could result in death. It may still result in death for Simeon, and they might all still die from starvation. The brothers understand all these things, but there's a more serious issue facing them. The brothers' fundamental fear is a fear of judgment for sin, and that from God Almighty!

All who sin without repentance and forgiveness carry a great burden. Pity the atheist, the secularist, the humanist—they have no mechanism for cleansing of the soul. They all are guilty of the folly of thinking that to not believe in something denies it the ability to exist. This is so common, and so obviously wrong! Pity the religious people also; they can only see a long list of commands they feel they must obey, but they have never ever been able to keep them all. Yet still they try, imagining that to merely try and fail will satisfy the law of God!

The brothers' problem is a burden of sin, which they are only now beginning to acknowledge among themselves. Their fear is that they are out of step with God. They are unable to fully articulate this, but it's growing clearer by the hour. This is the only explanation for their strange response to the even stranger bundles of money. *God is playing with us*, they may think. How wrong they are! At one level it has nothing to do with God. Joseph did it! But these men have seen through that. They know what they have done. They don't know what to do about it!

Note that here Jacob is reintroduced to the narrative with the brothers. They all stand together—in fear! A common fear does this; it unites people.

So what are we to make of Jacob's fear? Jacob is not afraid of the Lord. He does seem to have wandered away from his relationship with the God of his fathers. He doesn't turn to Him or call on Him. There are no angelic visitors or messengers to wrestle with over the problem. Why? Because Jacob has been worn down with problems in life. He's old, and he's given up on the struggle to walk with God. It's a sad picture. His interests and energy are all channelled into his family. Jacob is afraid of losing Benjamin and Simeon. But the real pain is surely the shock of it all. It brings back memories of the pain of losing Joseph. Jacob is not worried about food or foreign powers; he's just stuck in the practical reality of a hard life affecting his children. Parents still suffer pain with their children when they grow into adult life, maybe more pain! Jacob is afraid of losing his children, and it's an immediate threat.

Many readers will resonate with this depressing pain in Jacob. But you must not settle for this broken-parent syndrome! Before you react to this strong exhortation, remember or read to the end of the story that reunites them all. They even live together in the same area! Things go well in the end for them. They are about to be delivered out of famine into plenty and in the process be brought together so completely that they will be amazed.

Only God can do what is needed. All your worry and agonizing prayer can't accomplish it. God has a plan. Your prayers are a part of it, so keep on praying, but it doesn't depend on your praying; it's God's plan. Your prayers will change you, so don't stop. He's working it all out! Rejoice in His unfailing love. He loves your children too. You may lose them for a while, but if there's any improvement it will come from heaven. God restored all of Jacob's children to him. That's worth praying for. Live like you believe in such a good God with such a good purpose.

> *And Jacob their father said to them, "You have bereaved me: Joseph is no more, Simeon is no more, and you want to take Benjamin. All these things are against me."*
> —Genesis 42:36

Genesis 37:2 says, *"This is the history of Jacob."* Jacob was successful and rich and blessed at that time in his life. Now, Israel is an old man and has no power to do anything but cling to what he has and not let go. One wonders if, since the loss of Joseph, Israel has sunk into despair and forgotten the God of Bethel. We too can forget the days of God's goodness and let the bad days overwhelm us. Take courage here; God is still looking after Israel. He never stopped for a moment.

Providence is summed up in two words: foresight and provision. God saw what happened to Joseph. He saw the famine, brought the two together, and provided a saviour for Israel and his family in Joseph. How wrong we are to doubt God! Yet Jacob does. Have you never felt like he does here? *"All these things are against me."* Yet all these things are working out God's purposes. All these things are going to be brought to a good end.

> *Then Reuben spoke to his father, saying, "Kill my two sons if I do not bring him back to you; put him in my hands, and I will bring him back to you."*
> —Genesis 42:37

Reuben illustrates a common occurrence in situations of stress. People uncontrollably blurting out words without thought under the impulse of shock or nerves. This is desperation and blustering when stillness and thoughtfulness are required. Nobody here wants anybody to die! Reuben, first to speak, must feel that empty futile feeling we have when we make a big statement that's just ridiculous. Maybe it's his personality. Maybe it's a desperate attempt at reinstatement with his dad. Maybe it's another skeleton in Reuben's cupboard that's not been dealt with, twisting inside him. He probably feels responsible. Or perhaps it's just the oldest brother taking the lead. But he certainly says the wrong thing! He's trying to give assurance to Jacob. But the response from his father is emphatic.

> *But he said, "My son shall not go down with you, for his brother is dead, and he is left alone. If any calamity should befall him along the way in which you go, then you would bring down my gray hair with sorrow to the grave."*
> —Genesis 42:38

Note that Jacob still segregates the sons of Rachel from his other sons. He says, *"My son…his brother is dead, and he is left alone."* Note also that God doesn't separate them to the same degree. God is moving them together, not separating them, and they all will become the heads of the tribes of Israel.

chapter forty-three

PISTACHIO NUTS

Now the famine was severe in the land. And it came to pass, when they had eaten up the grain which they had brought from Egypt, that their father said to them, "Go back, buy us a little food." But Judah spoke to him, saying, "The man solemnly warned us, saying, "You shall not see my face unless your brother is with you.' If you send our brother with us, we will go down and buy you food. But if you will not send him, we will not go down; for the man said to us, "You shall not see my face unless your brother is with you."' And Israel said, "Why did you deal so wrongfully with me as to tell the man whether you had still another brother?" But they said, "The man asked us pointedly about ourselves and our family, saying, "Is your father still alive? Have you another brother?' And we told him according to these words. Could we possibly have known that he would say, "Bring your brother down'?" Then Judah said to Israel his father, "Send the lad with me, and we will arise and go, that we may live and not die, both we and you and also our little ones. I myself will be surety for him; from my hand you shall require him. If I do not bring him back to you and set him before you, then let me bear the blame forever. For if we had not lingered, surely by now we would have returned this second time." And their father Israel said to them, "If it must be so, then do this: Take some of the best fruits of the land in your vessels and carry down a present for the man—a

> *little balm and a little honey, spices and myrrh, pistachio nuts and almonds. Take double money in your hand, and take back in your hand the money that was returned in the mouth of your sacks; perhaps it was an oversight. Take your brother also, and arise, go back to the man. And may God Almighty give you mercy before the man, that he may release your other brother and Benjamin. If I am bereaved, I am bereaved!"*
>
> —Genesis 43:1–14

Ah, Israel! Unbelieving and miserable. Fatalistic and sad. A legitimate, if now inordinate, extended grief has become his *"being."* But it's founded upon lies! Unbelief rests comfortably upon lies. Unbelief believes! But it believes the wrong things. Israel is blinded by it and doesn't realize that the famine could kill them all. His sons have to point this out to him. But despite it all, God has a glorious end to the history of Jacob. He has an even more glorious end for you, believer, when Christ comes to take His people home.

"So the men took that present and Benjamin, and they took double money in their hand, and arose and went down to Egypt" (Genesis 43:15). They take lots of stuff, including honey and spices and pistachio nuts, to please Joseph, and they take Benjamin. We are so like them! When we approach the Lord we bring lots of stuff—the stuff of worship, the stuff of service, the stuff of good works. Joseph just wants to see Benjamin! He doesn't care about the "best fruits" of a land in famine; he has much better food in Egypt. He does want to see Benjamin!

So here again we can see that timeless human tendency for self-justification, always looking for a salvation based on our contribution. Be it ever so insignificant, it must have its place. "I will bring Benjamin...but not without my little bag of pistachio nuts." How blind, how pathetic, how foolish! Jesus Christ is all that God wants you to offer; not Jesus plus anything else—just Christ alone. Believe it, grasp it, take the cup of salvation—it's free!

Even as believers professing to be saved by grace, we revert to a Christian life based on good works. *"Having begun in the Spirit"* we imagine that we are *"now being made perfect by the flesh"* (Galatians 3:3). God wants none of it! But He does want us to bring our brother—that is, our estranged brother in the first place. Together, we are to bring Jesus. To talk to God about Jesus. To worship Jesus and extol Him and declare His beauty in worship. We are to bring Jesus and nothing else, not even ourselves. Certainly not our good works; they are like dried up pistachio nuts! God wants to see His children worship His Son.

chapter forty-four

BEING ASTONISHED

> *When Joseph saw Benjamin with them, he said to the steward of his house, "Take these men to my home, and slaughter an animal and make ready; for these men will dine with me at noon."*
> —Genesis 43:16

Joseph gives instant acceptance when they all come together. A feast is prepared, and Joseph joins them. What a glorious picture; what an awesome moment!

> *Then the man did as Joseph ordered, and the man brought the men into Joseph's house. Now the men were afraid because they were brought into Joseph's house; and they said, "It is because of the money, which was returned in our sacks the first time, that we are brought in, so that he may make a case against us and seize us, to take us as slaves with our donkeys."*
> —Genesis 43:17–18

They still don't get it. They think he's out to get them, to catch them out. Who gives strangers things for nothing? God does! The price has already been paid by Jesus. Come as you are and accept the free gift of salvation.

> *When they drew near to the steward of Joseph's house, they talked with him at the door of the house, and said,*

Being Joseph

> *"O sir, we indeed came down the first time to buy food; but it happened, when we came to the encampment, that we opened our sacks, and there, each man's money was in the mouth of his sack, our money in full weight; so we have brought it back in our hand. And we have brought down other money in our hands to buy food. We do not know who put our money in our sacks." But he said, "Peace be with you, do not be afraid. Your God and the God of your father has given you treasure in your sacks; I had your money." Then he brought Simeon out to them.*
> —Genesis 43:19–23

See this heathen Egyptian, pointing these sons of Abraham to the blessing of the God of Jacob, and he reminds them that He is their God too. It's your God who blessed you, he says. He says, *"I had your money."* This tends to suggest that Joseph's servants put Joseph's money into their sacks, leaving their payment with the steward.

> *So the man brought the men into Joseph's house and gave them water, and they washed their feet; and he gave their donkeys feed. Then they made the present ready for Joseph's coming at noon, for they heard that they would eat bread there. And when Joseph came home, they brought him the present which was in their hand into the house, and bowed down before him to the earth. Then he asked them about their well-being, and said, "Is your father well, the old man of whom you spoke? Is he still alive?"*
> —Genesis 43:24–27

These are intense moments for the brothers and for Joseph. They are worried about themselves, and Joseph is desperate to see Benjamin and hear about Israel.

> *And they answered, "Your servant our father is in good health; he is still alive." And they bowed their heads down*

> *and prostrated themselves. Then he lifted his eyes and saw his brother Benjamin, his mother's son, and said, "Is this your younger brother of whom you spoke to me?" And he said, "God be gracious to you, my son."*
> —Genesis 43:28–29

So far Joseph has kept up his distance and his act. The language here is inspired to tell us how precious Benjamin is to Joseph. *"He lifted his eyes"*—there's a moment of change here—*"And saw...'your younger brother of whom you spoke.'"* All these phrases reinforce the passion of the moment for Joseph. This is an intense emotional experience.

> *Now his heart yearned for his brother; so Joseph made haste and sought somewhere to weep. And he went into his chamber and wept there.*
> —Genesis 43:30

So intense is the emotion, the yearning, in Joseph's heart that this powerful ruler seeks a place to weep! The dam is breaking up!

> *Then he washed his face and came out; and he restrained himself, and said, "Serve the bread." So they set him a place by himself, and them by themselves, and the Egyptians who ate with him by themselves; because the Egyptians could not eat food with the Hebrews, for that is an abomination to the Egyptians.*
> —Genesis 43:31–32

Are we stretching this moment to say that it may remind us of the Lord's table? There the Lord says, *"Serve the bread."* He has wept for us; He has brought us to gather into His presence. He knows us; we can't know Him unless He reveals Himself to us. The Lord's Table is set for His own blood-bought brethren. The world has a table of its own, and we are not welcome there, but we are welcome here, even conscious of our sins, even still hiding in our sins. Yet He has set a table for us in His presence!

> *And they sat before him, the firstborn according to his birthright and the youngest according to his youth; and the men looked in astonishment at one another.*
> —Genesis 43:33

Astonishment is called for as they are at the table Joseph has prepared. We are likewise astonished at the table Jesus has prepared for us.

> *Then he took servings to them from before him, but Benjamin's serving was five times as much as any of theirs. So they drank and were merry with him.*
> —Genesis 43:34

Was this an alcoholic drink? Yes, it almost certainly was beer or wine. Beer was the staple drink in Ancient Egypt. Neither beer nor wine was very potent but sufficient to make them "merry." *Merry* is a word associated with the mild effect of alcohol.

Some suggest that wine and beer were used in preference to the polluted water of the Nile. They were used by adults and children alike so were not very potent at all. Wine was more associated with the wealthy, so the environment of this story in an Egyptian palace suggest they drank wine, or both. Drinking too much was frowned upon for the same reasons then as now.

Drinking reduces our sensibilities, removes our restraints, gives us a false feeling of freedom, and unquestionably makes a mockery of men made in the image of God. The Bible says nothing good about alcohol. Any thorough study reveals a very bad image about alcohol and those who drink it for pleasure. Nothing has changed; the Christian church has always held it as a bad thing. Today we can't drive a car after drinking more than a small amount because studies have shown the diminishing effect upon reason and comprehension it produces. The slowing of essential responses to danger, practical and moral, are well documented, but still many professing believers find an excuse to indulge, calling upon reasoning that defies logic to justify a mere "pleasure" at the expense of their testimony. Here, in the story of Joseph, it perhaps lightened the moment while they ate and were "merry."

chapter forty-five

BEING CONFUSED

> *And he commanded the steward of his house, saying, "Fill the men's sacks with food, as much as they can carry, and put each man's money in the mouth of his sack. Also put my cup, the silver cup, in the mouth of the sack of the youngest, and his grain money." So he did according to the word that Joseph had spoken. As soon as the morning dawned, the men were sent away, they and their donkeys.*
> —Genesis 44:1–3

As the morning dawned, a new day, the brothers wanted to get back home again as quickly as possible to get a break from this pressure. They had escaped. Perhaps they hoped they would never have to return!

> *When they had gone out of the city, and were not yet far off, Joseph said to his steward, "Get up, follow the men; and when you overtake them, say to them, 'Why have you repaid evil for good? Is not this the one from which my lord drinks, and with which he indeed practices divination? You have done evil in so doing.'" So he overtook them, and he spoke to them these same words.*
> —Genesis 44:4–6

How can we imagine the despair that must have filled their minds and hearts? Every one of them felt innocent yet proven guilty before they even objected. They could not understand what was happening to them or why. The accusation gets worse with each detail: that they repaid evil for good and stole Joseph's cup, which he drank from and also practiced divination with. It was overwhelming, and they felt wronged.

> *And they said to him, "Why does my lord say these words? Far be it from us that your servants should do such a thing. Look, we brought back to you from the land of Canaan the money which we found in the mouth of our sacks. How then could we steal silver or gold from your lord's house? With whomever of your servants it is found, let him die, and we also will be my lord's slaves." And he said, "Now also let it be according to your words; he with whom it is found shall be my slave, and you shall be blameless."*
> —Genesis 44:7–10

The more innocent they feel, the more they risk to prove it.

"*Then each man speedily let down his sack to the ground, and each opened his sack*" (Genesis 44:11). They willingly open their sacks, but God is trying to open their hearts. When we are hiding iniquity in our hearts, we will do anything but the thing that needs to be done. They are carrying around guilt that has become a part of who they are. They learned to live with it and thought they got away with it. Even now when they have been forced to reconsider and even among themselves confessed that selling Joseph may be the cause of this trouble, they can't make a straightforward confession to God.

> *So he searched. He began with the oldest and left off with the youngest; and the cup was found in Benjamin's sack. Then they tore their clothes, and each man loaded his donkey and returned to the city.*
> —Genesis 44:12–13

Years earlier they had torn Joseph's coat of many colours to support their lie. Now they tear their own clothing in contrite admission of defeat.

"*So Judah and his brothers came to Joseph's house, and he was still there; and they fell before him on the ground*" (Genesis 44:14). The most significant thing here is not the men falling before Joseph; it's the fulfillment of the dream that God gave Joseph. Here it is, the brothers prostrate before him.

> *And Joseph said to them, "What deed is this you have done? Did you not know that such a man as I can certainly practice divination?" Then Judah said, "What shall we say to my lord? What shall we speak? Or how shall we clear ourselves? God has found out the iniquity of your servants; here we are, my lord's slaves, both we and he also with whom the cup was found." But he said, "Far be it from me that I should do so; the man in whose hand the cup was found, he shall be my slave. And as for you, go up in peace to your father."*
>
> —Genesis 44:15–17

Joseph speaks as though they had done no wrong, so why would he hold them? They are innocent. Only the one who had the cup is guilty and needs to be his slave. He's quite happy to let them go back to Canaan if they leave Benjamin in captivity. He's testing them to see if they have really changed. Will they do to Benjamin what they did to him? Will they look after themselves and leave both Benjamin and Joseph in captivity as though dead?

Judah intervenes this time.

> *Then Judah came near to him and said: "O my lord, please let your servant speak a word in my lord's hearing, and do not let your anger burn against your servant; for you are even like Pharaoh. My lord asked his servants,*

> saying, 'Have you a father or a brother?' And we said to my lord, 'We have a father, an old man, and a child of his old age, who is young; his brother is dead, and he alone is left of his mother's children, and his father loves him.' Then you said to your servants, 'Bring him down to me, that I may set my eyes on him.' And we said to my lord, 'The lad cannot leave his father, for if he should leave his father, his father would die.' But you said to your servants, 'Unless your youngest brother comes down with you, you shall see my face no more.' So it was, when we went up to your servant my father, that we told him the words of my lord. And our father said, 'Go back and buy us a little food.' But we said, 'We cannot go down; if our youngest brother is with us, then we will go down; for we may not see the man's face unless our youngest brother is with us.'"
>
> —Genesis 44:18–26

Judah here is retelling the events without the time breaks that occurred. The story conveys the facts better when told complete. Then he gets to the present, and now Joseph doesn't know what to expect.

> "Then your servant my father said to us, 'You know that my wife bore me two sons; and the one went out from me, and I said, "Surely he is torn to pieces"; and I have not seen him since.'"
>
> —Genesis 44:27–28

Judah quotes his father, Jacob, in these words. The interesting thing is that Judah seems to believe that Joseph has died, even though he didn't kill him. It appears that although the brothers don't know what happened to Joseph, they have convinced themselves that he must be dead by now. One thing is certain: they have never told their father, Jacob, the true story.

"'But if you take this one also from me, and calamity befalls him, you shall bring down my gray hair with sorrow to the grave.' Now therefore, when I come to your servant my father, and the lad is not with us, since his life is bound up in the lad's life, it will happen, when he sees that the lad is not with us, that he will die. So your servants will bring down the gray hair of your servant our father with sorrow to the grave."
—Genesis 44:29–31

So having made the case against taking Joseph taking Benjamin into slavery, Judah now goes on to show the extent of the change that has taken place in him, indicating for us a change in them all.

"For your servant became surety for the lad to my father, saying, 'If I do not bring him back to you, then I shall bear the blame before my father forever.' Now therefore, please let your servant remain instead of the lad as a slave to my lord, and let the lad go up with his brothers. For how shall I go up to my father if the lad is not with me, lest perhaps I see the evil that would come upon my father?"
—Genesis 44:32–34

Here Judah speaks personally, showing his love for his father. This indicates to us a change of heart in them all, perhaps about all the events of their family life.

chapter forty-six

JOSEPH REVEALED

Then Joseph could not restrain himself before all those who stood by him, and he cried out, "Make everyone go out from me!" So no one stood with him while Joseph made himself known to his brothers.

—Genesis 45:1

Judah got through! One might ask whether Joseph is acting out a prepared plan or going with the flow spontaneously. He is undoubtedly in charge of events. He has more understanding of what is going on than anyone else. After all, he recognized his brothers; they still don't recognize him. Even when the Bible tells us *"Judah came near to him"* to speak with him (Genesis 44:18), he didn't recognize him. Joseph sees the overall picture; they are confused. He has set in motion everything that has happened. But there are a few areas where he's in the dark and they have the information.

They have shown him that Benjamin is alive. They have told him that their father is alive, but he has not seen Jacob. It seems that Joseph didn't trust them initially and took them through a number of tests to check their honesty. He seems satisfied now about that, but he has to check their heart attitude to Benjamin. Will they sacrifice Benjamin to get their freedom and leave him in Egypt?

Here Judah's entreaty for their father seems to have broken Joseph's hard exterior guard. Joseph examined Judah and found him to be genuine, and that penetrated to his heart and was the last straw, so to speak. Joseph is now convinced that everything is as it seems with them. He can't restrain himself any longer. He can't hide himself any more. The emotional dam—built initially many years earlier, added to as the years went by, and now weakened by the events of this story spanning a significant length of time—is bursting right now! The shock must have terrified, confused, and bewildered these lost brothers. This experience just gets stranger to them at every turn.

"And he wept aloud, and the Egyptians and the house of Pharaoh heard it" (Genesis 45:2). *"He wept"* would have indicated relief and emotional tiredness. But *"He wept aloud"* suggests a deeper feeling than mere relief. The emotional dam inside Joseph is bursting! Such long-term burdens seldom show themselves in public. They become silent permanent partners in life. Those who are carrying them feel their weight often, but others know nothing about them. When the problem is reversed in God's good timing, by His surprising deliverances, the weight of that burden bursts an emotional dam, and the deluge is felt by all those around. Often it's expressed in public. Many can't handle such emotions, but those who have walked with God see themselves in a past day. It's a bursting of pain and joy all mingled together. The pain of hurt and the relief of deliverance make good friends in this moment of release.

God keeps His Word. Trust is rewarded, and faith is justified. God is good.

Joseph simply breaks down and declares, *"I am Joseph."*

> *Then Joseph said to his brothers, "I am Joseph; does my father still live?" But his brothers could not answer him, for they were dismayed in his presence.*
> —Genesis 45:3

Oh, these poor men! He has been friend, foe, friend again, and now he is family! They can't speak. We can see their confusion and fear. What will happen now? They have been unable to predict or explain anything that has so far happened to them. What is this now?

Joseph Revealed

> *And Joseph said to his brothers, "Please come near to me." So they came near. Then he said: "I am Joseph your brother, whom you sold into Egypt."*
> —Genesis 45:4

"*Come near to me*" is such an endearing invitation, an invitation to get close and forget status and rules and protocols. Let's be brothers and get close! Hear also a hint of Jesus in John's Gospel after the crucifixion:

> *Jesus came…and stood in the midst, and said, "Peace to you!" Then He said to Thomas, "Reach your finger here, and look at My hands; and reach your hand here, and put it into My side. Do not be unbelieving, but believing."*
> —John 20:26–27

Jesus' words carry a gentle rebuke to doubting Thomas. Joseph's words carry no rebuke, being brother to brother. He says *"whom you sold into Egypt"* to identify himself, not to condemn them. Such love and grace!

> *"But now, do not therefore be grieved or angry with yourselves because you sold me here; for God sent me before you to preserve life."*
> —Genesis 45:5

Joseph here now shows them, and us, his true self. He offers no condemnation and only his belief that God was behind the whole thing for good! Even then God's people had difficulty believing this.

Paul in the New Testament has to remind the Lord's people that *"All things work together for good to those who love God, to those who are the called according to His purpose"* (Romans 8:28). Today many pastors struggle to convince dedicated believers of this truth because even we who live in the last days, with the whole Bible to take strength from, still fail to believe this truth. God is working even in the bad times. He has not deserted us even when it feels like and looks like He has!

> *"For these two years the famine has been in the land, and there are still five years in which there will be neither plowing nor harvesting. And God sent me before you to preserve a posterity for you in the earth, and to save your lives by a great deliverance. So now it was not you who sent me here, but God; and He has made me a father to Pharaoh, and lord of all his house, and a ruler throughout all the land of Egypt."*
>
> —Genesis 45:6–8

Joseph, like his mother before him, sees the whole of his life as the outworking of God's plan for his family, for Jacob and his sons. Did he see it before this day? It looks like he had some kind of insight, a little idea, a possible interpretation of his dreams. His brothers and his father had rushed in to give him the interpretation of his dream when he was young. But in the intervening years Joseph saw that both the big picture and the agricultural inference of the dream were relevant. "Sheaves" bowed down in his dreams. Through the years God must have been revealing more and more to Joseph. Today it all comes together in its entirety, so clearly that he declares it to his brothers. Then, in such a normal family way, he says, *"Hurry and go up to my father."*

> *"Hurry and go up to my father, and say to him, 'Thus says your son Joseph: "God has made me lord of all Egypt; come down to me, do not tarry."'"*
>
> —Genesis 45:9

Jacob's history is tied up in the life of his sons, as all of our lives are tied up in our children in one way or another. Jacob has lived long enough to see the day when his second youngest son can take care of the whole extended family and their flocks and herds! That is a blessed life.

> "'You shall dwell in the land of Goshen, and you shall be near to me, you and your children, your children's children, your flocks and your herds, and all that you have. There I will provide for you, lest you and your household, and all that you have, come to poverty; for there are still five years of famine.' And behold, your eyes and the eyes of my brother Benjamin see that it is my mouth that speaks to you. So you shall tell my father of all my glory in Egypt, and of all that you have seen; and you shall hurry and bring my father down here."
> —Genesis 45:10–13

Here is another little glimpse into the relationship between the Father and the Son that the believer should take to heart when worshipping or praying. When you approach God for any reason, here is where to begin and to stay for as long as possible. Joseph says, *"Tell my father of all my glory in Egypt, and of all that you have seen."* Tell the Lord that you understand that great humiliation, the incarnation, that was just the beginning of the saving work of God the Son. Tell the Lord how wonderful a life He lived on earth, doing good and healing all who were oppressed by the devil. Tell the Lord that you understand His conflicts with the religious leaders of society. Tell Him that you appreciate His great sadness over Israel's rejection of their own Messiah. Tell the Lord that you are ashamed of His mock trial, ashamed of the lies told about Him. Tell the Lord, with tears, that you have seen Him in your mind's eye in Pilate's hall being beaten by hardened, frustrated Roman soldiers, forced to keep the peace in this little place full of zealots. The zealots, with knifes under their outer tunics, thought they were serving God by killing the heathen who had occupied their land, God's land, the promised land. These soldiers took out their frustrations on the Lord Jesus

Christ! What must it have been like to have carried His cross on the road to the cross? Pray the following:

> Lord, I wish I could have sat there and watched with You, but I would have run away like the other disciples. I know that You rose again victorious over death and hell and that You are seated at Your Father's right hand in glory interceding for us, for me, for my sick friend and brother. Lord, touch him with that risen power and heal him and put modern medicine again into confusion!

Joseph says to his brothers, "Tell my father of all my glory in Egypt."

> Then he fell on his brother Benjamin's neck and wept, and Benjamin wept on his neck. Moreover he kissed all his brothers and wept over them, and after that his brothers talked with him.
> —Genesis 45:14–15

When the Bible says, *"his brothers talked with him,"* there's a sense of peace that is found nowhere in Joseph's dealings with his brothers before now. It has taken all these years of pain and trouble to bring them to this place. They have come together at last. Tears have been shed, pain has been expressed, and peace has settled. They talked together. What did they talk about? The Bible doesn't tell us the content, only the tone, of the conversation. Joseph kissed them and wept over them. Conversation born out of such affection is rich and memorable.

> Now the report of it was heard in Pharaoh's house, saying, "Joseph's brothers have come." So it pleased Pharaoh and his servants well.
> —Genesis 45:16

Even the world is a happier place when the church is walking with God and in harmony.

SECTION X: BEING RESTORED

chapter forty-seven

DON'T DIE BEFORE YOU'RE DEAD

The Bible says, *"When a man's ways please the LORD, He makes even his enemies to be at peace with him"* (Proverbs 16:7). In the following passage this is illustrated for us as Pharaoh takes control and tells Joseph to bring his father down to Egypt to stay.

> *And Pharaoh said to Joseph, "Say to your brothers, 'Do this: Load your animals and depart; go to the land of Canaan. Bring your father and your households and come to me; I will give you the best of the land of Egypt, and you will eat the fat of the land. Now you are commanded—do this: Take carts out of the land of Egypt for your little ones and your wives; bring your father and come. Also do not be concerned about your goods, for the best of all the land of Egypt is yours.'"*
>
> —Genesis 45:17–20

"Do not be concerned about your goods"—there's a piece of advice we could do well to heed in this materialistic day. God tells His children *"Do not worry about tomorrow"* (Matthew 6:34). But today that advice has been rejected in favour of insurance companies, advertising, banks, and a total capitalistic model for living. You are imagined to be spiritual if you have succeeded in the world! Since when was a large house, a cottage or two, and a new car every three years evidence of spirituality? God's ways are not our ways. Does a heathen ruler look after God's people better than He does? The actions of many Western Christians suggest that they believe a

bank manager is better than God. Jesus said, *"Do not worry."* Think of the time you spend thinking, worrying, about material things. Listen to this most basic gospel teaching: *"Your Father knows the things you have need of before you ask Him"* (Matthew 6:8).

See the provision the heathen king made for Joseph's family freely, willingly, and generously:

> *Then the sons of Israel did so; and Joseph gave them carts, according to the command of Pharaoh, and he gave them provisions for the journey. He gave to all of them, to each man, changes of garments; but to Benjamin he gave three hundred pieces of silver and five changes of garments. And he sent to his father these things: ten donkeys loaded with the good things of Egypt, and ten female donkeys loaded with grain, bread, and food for his father for the journey.*
> —Genesis 45:21–23

God has made ample provision for us, and we don't need to worry about anything regarding our daily needs.

"So he sent his brothers away, and they departed; and he said to them, 'See that you do not become troubled along the way'" (Genesis 45:24). Here is good advice for the Christian's daily walk: *"Do not become troubled along the way."* On our journey to heaven, our promised land, our Canaan, we will face many dangers and difficulties. Some will be of our own making; some will be attacks on our faith. The danger of disharmony among us on the way is great. All of these trials are sent by God or allowed by God, so don't be troubled about trouble! When it comes, deal with it thoroughly, or it will stay with you, like the mixed multitude that closely followed Israel in their journeys through the desert years. They were the source of lots of trouble for Israel. Or like Amalek, the nation God told Israel to utterly wipe out. They didn't do that, and Amalek fought, irritated, annoyed, and distracted Israel for generations. Amalek has been identified by some as representing the "flesh," that sinful principle of the old man, in its dying throes, warring against the new man in

Christ. Troubles will come; don't be troubled by them. Deal with them, with God. Then you will be singing *"along the way."*

But note that Joseph identifies the only real enemy they will have along the way to heaven—themselves! No external threat can overcome them; no enemy of their soul can bring them down. Their own private sins can't defeat them—they are forgiven and washed away—but they can be each other's greatest danger! Their walk together is only threatened by themselves. They must guard that relationship as they journey.

Journeying puts its own unique stresses on the traveller: tiredness, boredom, weariness, heat, cold, but most of all, personalities! Recriminations, irritations, arguments, emotions, recollections. Families fight; they must learn to forgive. How many families find Sunday mornings to be stressful? How often do families arrive at a worship service fighting? Make Sunday morning a special time together; don't be "troubled" on the way to the house of God.

Joseph warned them to be aware of this danger and to actively avoid it, work at it, not be discouraged, and deliberately defeat it. Don't be defeated by it!

It seems that the brothers took Joseph's advice to heart, as there's nothing noted about their journey back to Jacob. Perhaps they were reduced to silence by Joseph's love and forgiveness.

"Then they went up out of Egypt, and came to the land of Canaan to Jacob their father" (Genesis 45:25). The very language here is lighter and free and happy, so it seems that the journey home felt shorter for them this time. See that they *"went up out of Egypt."* This is always the way in the Old Testament language about Egypt, a place of descent and a place to escape out of, up to a higher plane of living, even though in this story and at this point in biblical history God was going to use Egypt to save His people.

> *And they told him, saying, "Joseph is still alive, and he is governor over all the land of Egypt." And Jacob's heart stood still, because he did not believe them.*
> —Genesis 45:26

Oh no! Not again! Jacob didn't believe them! How typical this family is of the Christian church! Jacob didn't believe; Israel, the prince with God, refused to believe! May God grant us a simple believing faith that trusts the word of our loving heavenly Father. Many of us will have similar experience when God moves in our circumstances to deliver us. *"Jacob's heart stood still"*—what a picture! A man whose heart beat for God now has his heart stop with shock at God's deliverances. Never get so far away from the Lord that His mercies stop your heart. Always keep your heart beating strongly in fellowship with Him. Then no situation, no news, be it ever so surprising, will affect your spiritual heartbeat.

> *But when they told him all the words which Joseph had said to them, and when he saw the carts which Joseph had sent to carry him, the spirit of Jacob their father revived.*
> —Genesis 45:27

Jacob revived! His energy returned, his zest for life returned, he saw a more positive future. But we are to read more here than mere physical and psychological effects. Jacob was, above all, a tired believer, a tired servant of God. In this moment of good news about his long-lost son, Joseph, that spirit of faith revived. His soul awakened. His joy in the Lord bubbled up again. His heart awakened and filled with the hope of the believer again.

What about you? Failing brother or sister, discouraged saint, don't give up! Look up! Look around you at God's provision, from the heavens above giving rain to the ground that produces harvests. From the body you reside in to your parents, your family, and the food on your table under a sound roof. From the energy that flows through your veins, the life in you, to the hope of eternal life in Jesus. From the sense of belonging to God's family to the knowledge of your sins forgiven. Look around you. See by the eye of faith the abundance of good things your loving heavenly Father has provided. See the unseen! Blessings await you in His good time. Go with the family of God to worship this week at the house of God. Sing

His praises with all the faith you can muster, and defy the flesh, the old man, and the misery of this world's talk. Read the word of life again, and fill your soul with good spiritual things.

"*Then Israel said, 'It is enough. Joseph my son is still alive. I will go and see him before I die'*" (Genesis 45:28). Make sure you do this! Make sure you see the Son, Jesus Christ, before you die! Make sure you know His forgiveness and have by faith received Him into your heart and received His Holy Spirit as the assurance of your eternal salvation.

And do the same for your family. If it's been a long time since you saw them, make sure you see them too before you die. End your days well. Finish well! Make a good sprint at the end, as much as you are able.

Also, don't wish for death or expect it too soon. Jacob said he would do this one last thing "before I die." Jacob lived another seventeen years! He had mourned for his son for around fifteen years, had wished he could see him again. He talked for hours about him over the months and years. He longed to see him again. Now that he was going to see him, he expected to see him one last time…and then drop dead! What madness does negativity produce in a human being? Not only had he wasted fifteen years mourning; he had written off the next seventeen years of his life before they began!

Many of us are just like Jacob. Live like you have a life before you. Don't let poor health or news or misery prevent you from serving God. The church is guilty of ageism and heading for a glamour model of the body of Christ. What blasphemy! God isn't interested in your age—it's only a number. So don't die before you're dead!

chapter forty-eight

SEEING VISIONS AGAIN

So Israel took his journey with all that he had.

—Genesis 46:1

What was Israel clinging to, *"all that he had"*? Joseph had said, *"Do not be concerned about your goods, for the best of all the land of Egypt is yours"* (Genesis 45:20). Don't bother with your old furniture and your bric-a-brac; you will be looked after when you get here.

Like Jacob, we cling, clutch, grab, hug, and hold on to stuff that is at best worthless, at worst a harmful distraction. Pilgrims travel light. Travellers are only hindered by excess baggage. A lot of it is material we can't take to heaven. Some of it is mental, troubles and tears we can't let go of. Yet like Jacob when we get to heaven we will see that it all had a good purpose! We keep lots of "things" because they give us a sense of worth or security. God wants us to trust in Him alone. Having "things" is okay, but trusting in them is a bit of a slap in the face to the Almighty!

"Israel...came to Beersheba, and offered sacrifices to the God of his father Isaac" (Genesis 46:1). This is where Abraham offered up Isaac. Did Jacob offer himself to the Lord here in this time of restoration?

"Then God spoke to Israel in the visions of the night, and said, 'Jacob, Jacob!'" (Genesis 46:2). Did the Lord have to repeat Himself because Jacob had not been listening for a while? The Lord had not forgotten his name. He has not forgotten yours either.

"And he said, 'Here I am'" (Genesis 46:2). Jacob's old spiritual sensitivity was not too far gone for him to respond as soon as he realized that the Lord was speaking to him. He said, *"Here I am"* like Isaiah would in Isaiah 6:8. Like the disciples would by the sea of Galilee, and every believer when they felt the force of irresistible grace. Will you now join them in saying in your heart *"Here I am"*?

> *So He said, "I am God, the God of your father; do not fear to go down to Egypt, for I will make of you a great nation there. I will go down with you to Egypt, and I will also surely bring you up again; and Joseph will put his hand on your eyes."*
>
> —Genesis 46:3–4

Here we can see how the history of Jacob was all tangled up in the life of Joseph, his son. All of this was in God's good providence. He knew the famine was coming. He looked after Jacob through Joseph and all his struggles.

"For I will make of you a great nation." Here we have a very common thing in the Bible, a little phrase that tells us that something will happen in the future. Four hundred years later, it did!

This is amazing evidence for the divine inspiration of the Scriptures. What is bewildering to the onlooker, to the angels, and to the cloud of witnesses is that when people claiming to be believers read these promises that have now been fulfilled, they express no amazement! They are no longer moved by God's almighty power to do what He says He will do.

More amazing still is that today we have difficulty believing that God can provide for our material needs without the aid of this world. God has proven Himself throughout the generations, and still we are filled with a comfortable unbelief. It's comfortable because unbelief stops us from taking the risks of faith and prevents us from being spiritual entrepreneurs. Unbelief reduces the church to a "safe house"! Or perhaps it's a comfortable belief in ourselves! Be careful! God might cut back on the help He had freely given despite our lack of prayer. He could also stop helping us altogether for a while until we discover again how useless we are at doing His work without Him. Of course as you read the Scriptures now, you could call upon the Name of the Lord and return to Him with all your heart!

Genesis 45:5–40 gives details of the family who went from Canaan to Goshen in Egypt with Israel. In all, there were seventy persons. As God promised, they became a great nation, and even to this day they are fundamental in world affairs. Abraham's descendants became like the sand on the seashore, like God promised they would (Genesis 22:17)!

chapter forty-nine

JACOB, BEING SETTLED

> *Then he sent Judah before him to Joseph, to point out before him the way to Goshen. And they came to the land of Goshen. So Joseph made ready his chariot and went up to Goshen to meet his father Israel; and he presented himself to him, and fell on his neck and wept on his neck a good while.*
>
> —Genesis 46:28–29

Joseph wept on his father's neck. The dam had burst; here the emotional flow is still so strong that it lasted *"a good while."* Joseph was experiencing the most essential healthy healing here with his father, Jacob, in their reunion.

"And Israel said to Joseph, 'Now let me die, since I have seen your face, because you are still alive'" (Genesis 46:30). The believer can say with quiet confidence to Jesus, "I can comfortably die, now that I know you are alive." Don't cling too strongly to this world. Jesus is waiting for us. When the evil days come, learn to loosen your grip. Learn to look forward when you think this world's road is ending, and see that a whole new highway is about to open up before you.

> *Then Joseph said to his brothers and to his father's household, "I will go up and tell Pharaoh, and say to him, 'My brothers and those of my father's house, who were in the land of Canaan, have come to me. And the men are shepherds, for their occupation has been to feed livestock; and*

> *they have brought their flocks, their herds, and all that they have.' So it shall be, when Pharaoh calls you and says, 'What is your occupation?' that you shall say, 'Your servants' occupation has been with livestock from our youth even till now, both we and also our fathers,' that you may dwell in the land of Goshen; for every shepherd is an abomination to the Egyptians."*
>
> —Genesis 46:31–34

Randy Alcorn tells us that in the ancient world shepherds were highly esteemed. Then this Egyptian view spread, and gradually, over the centuries, the work of the shepherd became less than respectable, often associated with the poor and even tainted with dishonesty.[7] By Jesus' time shepherds were the poorest and least in society, but He elevated them, making them the first messengers of the Good News of the gospel. He is called the good shepherd (John 10:11, 14), and Christ's ministers in His church have been given that name too. They are the shepherds whom God has set over the flock of God. The term now carries a respectable air of gentleness and caring.

> *Then Joseph went and told Pharaoh, and said, "My father and my brothers, their flocks and their herds and all that they possess, have come from the land of Canaan; and indeed they are in the land of Goshen." And he took five men from among his brothers and presented them to Pharaoh.*
>
> —Genesis 47:1–2

How to present yourself to a king? There are eleven brothers; how do you choose five?

In presenting yourself before the King of heaven, you would be well received if you were to identify yourself with these five points of Calvinism, referred to as TULIP:

---

[7] Randy Alcorn, "Shepherd Status," in *Come, Thou Long-Expected Jesus*, ed. Nancy Guthrie (Wheaton, IL: Crossway Books, 2008), 85–89.

T: Total Depravity. "Lord, I am a sinner." No believer would have difficulty in acknowledging this with tears.

U: Unconditional Election. What believer would not willing declare "Why me, Lord? There's nothing good in me"?

L: Limited Atonement. No believer would think that the atonement of Christ was insufficient. It was perfect, but its application is limited.

I: Irresistible Grace. No believer has found that he or she could resist the grace of God.

P: Perseverance of the Saints. All believers find themselves upheld and restored always, and if they stray they eventually return to the narrow road that leads to life. They persevere, by the help of the Holy Spirit.

Present these five statements as your testimony at the gate of heaven, and you will be recognized as a believer. Of course there are lots of simpler ways to present yourself and lots of different ways to express these same truths!

But here Joseph presents his family by presenting five brothers. If your church was looking for five people to be presented to a king, would the pastor choose you? Would you choose the pastor?

Isn't it interesting that the Bible doesn't tell us who they were? We would love to know, but they were now all equally brothers. What an egalitarian image it presents! Despite their differences, they were one family, all equal members. The very notion of favouritism seems to have disappeared from the narrative. See this amazing thing: When we are told that Joseph presented only five of the brothers, we don't feel like the others were absent! Somehow these men are now so united as twelve brothers that any five will completely represent them. This, only God can accomplish. Oh Lord, make us one!

Then Pharaoh said to his brothers, "What is your occupation?" And they said to Pharaoh, "Your servants are

> *shepherds, both we and also our fathers." And they said to Pharaoh, "We have come to dwell in the land, because your servants have no pasture for their flocks, for the famine is severe in the land of Canaan. Now therefore, please let your servants dwell in the land of Goshen." Then Pharaoh spoke to Joseph, saying, "Your father and your brothers have come to you. The land of Egypt is before you. Have your father and brothers dwell in the best of the land; let them dwell in the land of Goshen. And if you know any competent men among them, then make them chief herdsmen over my livestock." Then Joseph brought in his father Jacob and set him before Pharaoh; and Jacob blessed Pharaoh. Pharaoh said to Jacob, "How old are you?" And Jacob said to Pharaoh, "The days of the years of my pilgrimage are one hundred and thirty years; few and evil have been the days of the years of my life, and they have not attained to the days of the years of the life of my fathers in the days of their pilgrimage." So Jacob blessed Pharaoh, and went out from before Pharaoh.*
> —Genesis 47:3–10

We are seeing the old saint returning to his former self here. Jacob is not afraid anymore, not weak anymore, not even miserable anymore! The Lord had appeared to him along the way (Genesis 46:2–4). He blesses Pharaoh. Does Pharaoh feel any need of anything from this old saint? Probably not. But does Pharaoh actually need the prayers of the believer? Absolutely! Jacob here shows us the confidence of faith. He doesn't ask permission to bless; he assumes that the benefit is needed and will be conferred. This solid conviction is what strengthens people to witness to strangers.

> *And Joseph situated his father and his brothers, and gave them a possession in the land of Egypt, in the best of the land, in the land of Rameses, as Pharaoh had commanded. Then Joseph provided his father, his brothers, and all*

Jacob, Being Settled

> *his father's household with bread, according to the number in their families.*
>
> —Genesis 47:11–12

Joseph Deals with the Famine

> *Now there was no bread in all the land; for the famine was very severe, so that the land of Egypt and the land of Canaan languished because of the famine. And Joseph gathered up all the money that was found in the land of Egypt and in the land of Canaan, for the grain which they bought; and Joseph brought the money into Pharaoh's house. So when the money failed in the land of Egypt and in the land of Canaan, all the Egyptians came to Joseph and said, "Give us bread, for why should we die in your presence? For the money has failed."*
>
> —Genesis 47:13–15

Here we have a quiet reminder to those who put their trust in money for their security: Money can fail! Ask yourself, Christian, what you would do if you had no money. Of course nobody ever thinks it will happen to them. It can be just a few years from feast to famine. You would sell your house, your car, your cottage. Then what? See what they do:

> *Then Joseph said, "Give your livestock, and I will give you bread for your livestock, if the money is gone." So they brought their livestock to Joseph, and Joseph gave them bread in exchange for the horses, the flocks, the cattle of the herds, and for the donkeys. Thus he fed them with bread in exchange for all their livestock that year. When that year had ended, they came to him the next year and said to him, "We will not hide from my lord that our money is gone; my lord also has our herds of livestock. There*

is nothing left in the sight of my lord but our bodies and our lands."

—Genesis 47:16–18

Human beings can cope with incredible hardships when they are forced to. This has happened in societies since time began. Fortunes, as we call them carelessly, can be reversed! Will it take that to bring us to our knees?

"Why should we die before your eyes, both we and our land? Buy us and our land for bread, and we and our land will be servants of Pharaoh; give us seed, that we may live and not die, that the land may not be desolate." Then Joseph bought all the land of Egypt for Pharaoh; for every man of the Egyptians sold his field, because the famine was severe upon them. So the land became Pharaoh's. And as for the people, he moved them into the cities, from one end of the borders of Egypt to the other end. Only the land of the priests he did not buy; for the priests had rations allotted to them by Pharaoh, and they ate their rations which Pharaoh gave them; therefore they did not sell their lands. hen Joseph said to the people, "Indeed I have bought you and your land this day for Pharaoh. Look, here is seed for you, and you shall sow the land. And it shall come to pass in the harvest that you shall give one-fifth to Pharaoh. Four-fifths shall be your own, as seed for the field and for your food, for those of your households and as food for your little ones." So they said, "You have saved our lives; let us find favor in the sight of my lord, and we will be Pharaoh's servants." And Joseph made it a law over the land of Egypt to this day, that Pharaoh should have one-fifth, except for the land of the priests only, which did not become Pharaoh's

—Genesis 47:19–26

The people were grateful to the pharaoh for saving their lives, so they thankfully and willingly gave one-fifth of their produce. If believers universally gave even half of this amount, one-tenth, the church would have enough money to supply the world with Bibles and gospel literature and good deeds. That is of course if we didn't squander it on buildings, sound systems, and state of the art kitchens for ourselves. God, deliver us from materialism!

Note that the priests had a measure of preferential treatment and missed some of the extremes of the famine effects. Every society in history has had a priestly class. Every nation had gods, and their gods had human teachers and spokespeople. They were always treated with a unique respect. This was a mark of respect for their god. Generally they were a benefit to the society.

The history of religion is overall a respectable and honourable history. Its function was to give men a sense of security and a source of hope and protection, justice even, in a world of pain. It generally had in it some promise of an afterlife with family and friends. Some religions, of course, were satanic in every way, and all that the ideal religion offered was reversed in them. The fair treatment of all people in the afterlife of most religions was turned upside down and made to be a promise of licentiousness and lust and oppression. Universally they failed to provide a real and lasting value because they were based upon the insubstantial ideas of wicked, insubstantial men! However, the universal existence and persistence of religion as a fundamental part of human makeup tells us something about us. We need a focus outside of ourselves, something bigger and better, something powerful, someone who cares and looks out for us, someone we can approach and talk to.

The best definition of *religion* is "man searching for God." So what's different about Christianity? It's not man seeking God; it's the revelation given to mankind, in the Bible, that God is seeking us! He sent His Son to reveal Himself to us and to redeem us because we were so helpless that we were unable to help ourselves. And although Christianity is broadly accepted as a "religion," it's fundamentally different in its character and expression. It made the

Western world what it was when it was great. Any historian would be able to show a direct connection between the demise of sense and the rejection of Christianity in the Western world.

What is it about twenty-first-century men and women that they, above all others throughout the history of the human race, think they have need of nothing and care for nothing but their own tiny and irrelevant existence? They are totally antagonistic to the notion of anything or anyone bigger than themselves. Yet they are in a bigger mess than the rest of history put together! Empty in the extreme, needing drugs and alcohol and entertainment and diversions. Afraid of a free moment in which to look at themselves and see themselves as they truly are in reality. They are not important, not a saviour of a planet and not able to save themselves, not able to control their most basic passions. Who cares about putting robots on Mars? Twenty-first-century humans are no bigger than any before them. They seem to be, but that's an illusion. They are standing on the shoulders of centuries of really great people whom they now laugh at. They were, almost to a person, believers in a supreme being!

People today are ruining the only place they have to live. An angry universe is waiting to devour them in events surprisingly similar to the biblical descriptions of hell. A burning, disintegrating inferno—that is their own secular view. Pity them! They can't cope with an angry universe; how will they cope when the light dawns upon them that the angry universe is hiding an angry creator!

chapter fifty

BEING IN GOSHEN

So Israel dwelt in the land of Egypt, in the country of Goshen; and they had possessions there and grew and multiplied exceedingly. And Jacob lived in the land of Egypt seventeen years. So the length of Jacob's life was one hundred and forty-seven years. When the time drew near that Israel must die, he called his son Joseph and said to him, "Now if I have found favor in your sight, please put your hand under my thigh, and deal kindly and truly with me. Please do not bury me in Egypt."
—Genesis 47:27–29

The time has come that Israel *"must die."* God has set such a time for every one of us. Our time to die. We don't want to think about it. We want to believe that it's always far away. Some think it will never come; some wish it would come quicker than it does. Most of us really never want it to arrive. But it will!

Why does Jacob seem to handle death with so little drama? Death doesn't threaten him as though it was a spectre from the unknown beyond the grave. It's merely the door to heaven for Jacob. He knows God, he knows that God is his Father, and he's not afraid to meet Him. Many of the old saints, biblical and historical, show this same spirit. Death is neither an unknown nor a terror to those who walk with God. But Jacob is not so calm about where he will be buried! He says, *"Please do not bury me in Egypt, but let me lie with my fathers; you shall carry me out of Egypt and bury me in their burial place"* (Genesis 47:30).

It's a significant comfort to many of us to know that we'll be buried where our fathers are buried. It is, of course, only a comfort while we live. It's as though we hope to have their company after we die. There's also a sense, a kind of wish, for continuity with them. These like many other things have been commonly understood either as thoroughly Christian, as in a hope of heaven and reuniting with family and friends, or as a kind of semi-superstition. It's more a simple, common human experience but not necessarily wrong. Despite secularism, people still travel the world at great expense to fulfill the wish of a deceased parent or relative to be buried at their place of birth or where their partner is buried or with their parents. It presents some interesting issues when the parents are buried on two continents. This rare but not insignificant issue raises ridiculous questions for grandchildren. One thing is for certain: it's a human need to know where you will be buried. To know where your family or loved one is buried is another basic human need and essential sometimes for closure. To be able to visit a grave is an enormous benefit to bereaved families, which is why graveyards, the world over, for centuries, have been held sacrosanct and hallowed.

Jacob has a clear sense of what he wants and what he certainly does not want. It could be summed up in the word *identification*. He doesn't want to be identified with the heathen. He does want to be totally identified with his fathers. This we understand in Jacob's case to be a matter of family and also a matter of faith.

Many believer today seem to have no spiritual concern or thought as to these matters. They just go along with the doubtful advice of a funeral director. Speak to an educated pastor before you organize any funeral. He will have given it thorough study and thought.

"And he said, 'I will do as you have said'" (Genesis 47:30). Joseph's response shows no surprise, and we can assume that he has a similar understanding and faith. This seems to have persisted despite years in a foreign and unbelieving world.

"Then he said, 'Swear to me.' And he swore to him. So Israel bowed himself on the head of the bed" (Genesis 47:31). Jacob requires an oath, showing how serious this identification with his

fathers in death is to him. Joseph gives an instant assurance that the request will be carried out.

SECTION XI:
REST

chapter fifty-one

BEING BLESSED

Now it came to pass after these things that Joseph was told, "Indeed your father is sick"; and he took with him his two sons, Manasseh and Ephraim. And Jacob was told, "Look, your son Joseph is coming to you"; and Israel strengthened himself and sat up on the bed. Then Jacob said to Joseph: "God Almighty appeared to me at Luz in the land of Canaan and blessed me, and said to me, 'Behold, I will make you fruitful and multiply you, and I will make of you a multitude of people, and give this land to your descendants after you as an everlasting possession.' And now your two sons, Ephraim and Manasseh, who were born to you in the land of Egypt before I came to you in Egypt, are mine; as Reuben and Simeon, they shall be mine. Your offspring whom you beget after them shall be yours; they will be called by the name of their brothers in their inheritance. But as for me, when I came from Padan, Rachel died beside me in the land of Canaan on the way, when there was but a little distance to go to Ephrath; and I buried her there on the way to Ephrath (that is, Bethlehem)."

—Genesis 48:1–7

The biblical narrative has brought us full circle here in recounting the events of Jacob's life when Joseph was a child, up to the birth of Benjamin. The tone of Jacob's language is much more spiritually alert again. Since the Dinah incident, Jacob has been weak and recognizably less of the man he was in his earlier life. Now he seems to have been drawn close to the Lord again, and his thoughts are towards God. He has remembered days gone by and God's dealings. This is one of the healthiest things that you as a believer can do, to recount God's dealings in your life. You can do this in prayer to the Lord or tell your children or your friends. Remembering the days of God's blessing and His workings in you will bless your soul and all who listen. If you don't have anything to say on this subject, it's never too late to prove God. Seek Him now!

In the following family moments we can see that Jacob has returned to the status of a patriarch. He once again stands with Abraham and Isaac, his father and grandfather. Oh that God would raise up our children to stand where we have stood in our best days of walking with the living God! Jacob now speaks on behalf of his ancestors in blessing his children with God's blessings, which last forever.

> *Then Israel saw Joseph's sons, and said, "Who are these?" And Joseph said to his father, "They are my sons, whom God has given me in this place." And he said, "Please bring them to me, and I will bless them." Now the eyes of Israel were dim with age, so that he could not see. Then Joseph brought them near him, and he kissed them and embraced them. And Israel said to Joseph, "I had not thought to see your face; but in fact, God has also shown me your offspring!" So Joseph brought them from beside his knees, and he bowed down with his face to the earth. And Joseph took them both, Ephraim with his right hand toward Israel's left hand, and Manasseh with his left hand toward Israel's right hand, and brought them near him. Then Israel stretched out his right hand and laid it on Ephraim's head, who was the younger, and his left hand on Manasseh's head, guiding his hands knowingly, for Manasseh was the firstborn. And he blessed Joseph, and said: "God, before whom my fathers Abraham and Isaac walked, The God who has fed me all my life long to this day, The Angel*

who has redeemed me from all evil, Bless the lads; Let my name be named upon them, And the name of my fathers Abraham and Isaac; And let them grow into a multitude in the midst of the earth." Now when Joseph saw that his father laid his right hand on the head of Ephraim, it displeased him.

—Genesis 48:8–17

Joseph is *"displeased"*? Joseph, the man of peace, the innocent, gentle, caring man, is upset about something! Immediate family matters touch us deeper than most other things do. They often reveal a different side of us from the one we present in daily life. Jacob himself understands more than most the importance of inheritance and blessings and priority due to age. Had he not reversed this on his brother, Esau, and his own father, Isaac? Had he not suffered for this sin in running away like a fugitive for years? Yet he follows his instinctive grasp of the moment. He goes with his senses in this matter. Joseph is upset, displeased. He challenges his father. He sees discomfort already brewing in his family like in Jacob's family and tries to intervene:

So he took hold of his father's hand to remove it from Ephraim's head to Manasseh's head. And Joseph said to his father, "Not so, my father, for this one is the firstborn; put your right hand on his head." But his father refused and said, "I know, my son, I know. He also shall become a people, and he also shall be great; but truly his younger brother shall be greater than he, and his descendants shall become a multitude of nations."

—Genesis 48:17–19

Jacob's response shows that he knows how Joseph feels. He says, *"I know, I know."* Can you feel the understanding in Jacob here? Twice he reassures Joseph of a good outcome. God is like this. God gives us the Holy Spirit as an assurance that He will deliver on

His salvation promises. God knows us. He reads every breath; He feels every fear. Every moment of discomfort registers in His heart, and He feels for us. Never doubt this: He will deliver us and take us home to be with Himself.

> *So he blessed them that day, saying, "By you Israel will bless, saying, 'May God make you as Ephraim and as Manasseh!'" And thus he set Ephraim before Manasseh. Then Israel said to Joseph, "Behold, I am dying, but God will be with you and bring you back to the land of your fathers. Moreover I have given to you one portion above your brothers, which I took from the hand of the Amorite with my sword and my bow."*
> —Genesis 48:20–22

The Amorites were a vicious, powerful, and wicked nation and a significant society for 500 years until Moab subdued them. We are reminded here that Jacob was a man of God, a follower of the Lord God of Abraham, Isaac, and Jacob, and he was a warrior, fighting to defend his family and inheritance. God blessed him and them with tremendous success in battle.

Would to God that we did not have to fight! Would to God that war would end. But if the twentieth century has taught us little else, it taught us that while men are on the earth there will be wars and rumours of wars. Heaven—there are no wars there! The talk of wars in heaven is anthropomorphic. The actual event is indescribable to humans, but we only need a hint. God doesn't have to explain Himself to us.

When will the world realize how insignificant it is? And yet God so loved the world that He gave His only Son—try to grasp that! Someone said, "It's not what I don't understand about the Bible that puzzles me; it's what I do understand that puzzles me," meaning, "I understand the sinfulness of men met by the love of God in Jesus Christ on Calvary's cross! His forgiveness. His acceptance of us as we are."

How can God forgive sinners? The Bible gives us the answer, but it's so amazingly wonderful that it can be described as "unbelievable." The Cross of Calvary is the end of discussions about the where, why, when, and how of things. It's the beginning of discussions about God and me. The cross is the centre of the spiritual cosmos!

We want to avoid any discussion that comes close to exposing our sinful nature. We love to discuss the problems of the universe or the government or "that man over there." We even have the audacity to discuss God Himself with impatient critical analysis. But our discussion ends abruptly when the spotlight of reason and the light of truth begin to focus on ourselves. Mankind as a class, people as individuals, and me myself alone are all struck dumb when the truth about ourselves is placed centre stage to be discussed by the Judge of all the earth. Yet that discussion will be the most gentle, the most appealing, the most merciful and kind, offering peace and goodwill towards men, forgiveness and cleansing, and a new life in Jesus Christ.

God wants to start the discussion right here at the cross, with me, with you. He wants you to reason together with Him about this amazing topic. Reason with Him today about this question: What was going on at the cross? Why did an all-powerful and all-loving God send His Son to die for sinners, for the likes of me? These are among the greatest questions for a human being to ponder, and the most productive answer are available to all those who seek Him and find Him and are found by Him.

chapter fifty-two

CLOSING FAMILY MATTERS

So the family settles, reunited, in Goshen, a very fertile and wealthy land in Egypt. Jacob is there for seventeen years. He comes to his death and lays his hands on his family to bless them as his last act. Our interest in closing this story is the blessings for Joseph. We have seen the blessing of Joseph's life on everyone else. He lays no burden even on his enemies. Yet he is burdened by everyone with whom he comes into contact.

Jacob's opening statement for Joseph says, *"Joseph is a fruitful bough, a fruitful bough by a well; his branches run over the wall"* (Genesis 49:22). A fruitful vine requires pruning. Joseph's whole life was one of pruning by God to make him fruitful.

Don't despise God's cuttings. His pruning, His reducing of your size, is bringing you to nothing. He removes dead branches, clearing from your life everything that does not lead to fruit bearing. Make sure you belong to a good Bible-believing church where the pastoral preaching makes you uncomfortable with living in mediocrity. A comfortable church is half a church. Revelation tells us that half-hearted believers make God vomit (Revelation 3:16)! The truth is not always pleasant to listen to or read, but it's good for us!

Joseph's branches go over a wall. A Spirit-filled church can't remain internal, introverted, or self-satisfied. It sends its branches outside of itself, *"over the wall."* God has filled real believers with a desire to grow beyond their limits, over walls that contain and limit and restrict. The backslidden church stops at any old hurdle. It quits and shuts down and says, "Oh well, it's too big to scale." The people of God rise to challenges. They rise above walls. They jump over walls; they thrive on overcoming walls. Churches should give birth to churches as naturally as a mother bears children. God expects life to produce life. Multiplying churches is a healthier exercise than building mega-churches! Yet we don't despise large churches. Both large and small churches have blessings and problems.

"*The archers have bitterly grieved him, shot at him and hated him*" (Genesis 49:23). This is just Joseph's life. He was attacked with hostility. Oh God, make us like Joseph. As the sun rises consistently every day, let us arise to serve You. Let us arise to shine the gospel light and warmth everywhere. When we feel threatened, help us to put on the armour of God. There with that shield, though the archers shoot and though their arrows hit our shield, they will not hurt us.

> "*But his bow remained in strength, and the arms of his hands were made strong by the hands of the Mighty God of Jacob (from there is the Shepherd, the Stone of Israel).*"
> —Genesis 49:24

Steady, this strong characteristic that we get only by grace—let it identify us Lord. Keep us ready and steadily consistent, spiritually and mentally and physically fit to serve, always predictable in our service, in standing for truth, in being faithful no matter the consequences, always attributing the good things in our life to the Shepherd, the *"Stone of Israel."*

> "*By the God of your father who will help you, and by the Almighty who will bless you with blessings of heaven above, blessings of the deep that lies beneath, blessings of the breasts and of the womb.*"
> —Genesis 49:25

Lord, keep our children walking in our footsteps inasmuch as we have been faithful to You. Protect them from our failings. Give them heights of the experience of Your Spirit. Give them experiences that deepen them to reach springs of living water. Bless them with many children who are named with fruitful names, and likewise honour them. Make them a lifelong blessing.

> *"The blessings of your father have excelled the blessings of my ancestors, up to the utmost bound of the everlasting hills. They shall be on the head of Joseph, and on the crown of the head of him who was separate from his brothers."*
> —Genesis 49:26

Lord, grant our children Your blessings, which are more solid than the ancient rock, and to understand truths more durable than ages-old rock. Let Your blessings rest upon them in their minds and hearts and rest there until their lives are ended, fixed on the *"Rock of Ages."*

chapter fifty-three

JACOB DYING

Jacob's Death and Burial

"*Then he charged them and said to them: 'I am to be gathered to my people'*" (Genesis 49:29). What a lovely picture of dying!

> "*Bury me with my fathers in the cave that is in the field of Ephron the Hittite, in the cave that is in the field of Machpelah, which is before Mamre in the land of Canaan, which Abraham bought with the field of Ephron the Hittite as a possession for a burial place. There they buried Abraham and Sarah his wife, there they buried Isaac and Rebekah his wife, and there I buried Leah. The field and the cave that is there were purchased from the sons of Heth.*"
> —Genesis 49:29–32

Tenney makes an interesting observation on the subject of burial. He says, "It is remarkable that although God had given to Abraham the deed of the land of Canaan (Gen. 15:18–21), the only land that the patriarchs possessed before Joshua's time was the burial places for the original family: a cave at Hebron and a field at Shechem."[8]

While it is legitimate to own things in this life, including land, this is perhaps a healthy reminder that the only permanent possession we will be left with in this world, with any certainty, is our burial place, our grave. This should help us to hold the things of

---

8 Tenney, *Zondervan's Pictorial Bible Dictionary*, 232.

this world lightly and look forward to a more certain happier possession, our eternal home, in heaven.

> *And when Jacob had finished commanding his sons, he drew his feet up into the bed and breathed his last, and was gathered to his people. Then Joseph fell on his father's face, and wept over him, and kissed him.*
> —Genesis 49:33–50:1

We are regularly faced with the ambitions of fathers for their sons. Sons also have hopes and expectations of their fathers, though they are less often verbalized. In this passage we are privy to the final expression of the love and admiration of a son for his father, expressed with spontaneity. A moment of truth, private, deeply personal, yet for all to see. Fathers, here is a moment for us to live for. That day when the sum of our years will be measured in tears shed by our offspring. Here, uniquely expressed in the relationship of father to son. But also note in the following verse that Joseph remains in control of his affairs. He organizes what needs to be done. This is one measure of the extent of legitimate grief.

> *And Joseph commanded his servants the physicians to embalm his father. So the physicians embalmed Israel. Forty days were required for him, for such are the days required for those who are embalmed; and the Egyptians mourned for him seventy days. Now when the days of his mourning were past...*
> —Genesis 50:2–4

Days of mourning pass. Days of mourning must pass. Mourning here is measured in days. No doubt the loss was felt for much longer. But this being a much-loved and significant old man whose beloved wife had gone before him, the sad, heavy, bewildering kind of mourning of his family would have been for a minimal, normal, length of time.

Jacob Dying

Joseph spoke to the household of Pharaoh, saying, "If now I have found favor in your eyes, please speak in the hearing of Pharaoh, saying, 'My father made me swear, saying, "Behold, I am dying; in my grave which I dug for myself in the land of Canaan, there you shall bury me." Now therefore, please let me go up and bury my father, and I will come back.'" And Pharaoh said, "Go up and bury your father, as he made you swear." So Joseph went up to bury his father; and with him went up all the servants of Pharaoh, the elders of his house, and all the elders of the land of Egypt, as well as all the house of Joseph, his brothers, and his father's house. Only their little ones, their flocks, and their herds they left in the land of Goshen. And there went up with him both chariots and horsemen, and it was a very great gathering. Then they came to the threshing floor of Atad, which is beyond the Jordan, and they mourned there with a great and very solemn lamentation. He observed seven days of mourning for his father.

—Genesis 50:4–10

chapter fifty-four

BEING WATCHED... MOURNING

And when the inhabitants of the land, the Canaanites, saw the mourning at the threshing floor of Atad, they said, "This is a deep mourning of the Egyptians." Therefore its name was called Abel Mizraim, which is beyond the Jordan. So his sons did for him just as he had commanded them. For his sons carried him to the land of Canaan, and buried him in the cave of the field of Machpelah, before Mamre, which Abraham bought with the field from Ephron the Hittite as property for a burial place.

—Genesis 50:11–13

We appear to have become unhappy with *"mourning."* We have listened to the world. They have good reason to avoid the subject of death. For them it speaks of no hope. They have therefore turned it on its head and renamed mourning a "celebration of life." Life should be celebrated throughout its allotted span. Death must be acknowledged, faced up to, dealt with honestly, and mourned. It's "the last enemy." We do nothing for the world and posterity by ignoring its reality. It's seldom helpful to ignore a problem! Death is without doubt a problem to us all, believer and unbeliever.

The church must learn how to mourn again. We can learn how to mourn again at the Lord's Table. Be there regularly and thereby develop a truthful and honest way of handling bereavement. The Lord's table is a place where we look again at the sufferings of Christ for us. We acknowledge His death as a real death. We grasp something of the enormity of His sacrifice for us by staring at the cross for a while, not rushing away!

The original Lord's Table was a relaxed meal followed by a short intervention on the part of Jesus before He and the disciples went to the Mount of Olives. It was not protracted or drawn out. It was not intensely weepy, but it was significantly effective in sobering the disciples. They asked about their personal standing with the Lord Jesus: *"Lord, is it I?"* (Matthew 26:22). How bereft they would have been to not have asked that question! How robbed to not have had a moment of personal deep review of their relationship to Him who loved them! Note that they sang a hymn (Matthew 26:30). They left on a lighter note after a sober moment of unity in all its facets—purity, oneness, simplicity, unmixed, independent, satisfied, focused. Oneness, like in *"The LORD our God, the LORD is one!"* (Deuteronomy 6:4).

This mourning at the Lord's Table doesn't preclude joy and rejoicing. However, the joy expressed is unquestionably and clearly directed to the subject of the death and resurrection of Christ. We do not feature in that joy other than to be the ones expressing it. It's not about the fact that we are happy; it's about Him and only Him. We see no man except Jesus. But we don't fall into the error of forgetting the involvement of God the Father and God the Holy Spirit with God the Son, together working out our salvation.

The world is drawn to making comment on this mourning of God's people. The church must never forget that it is on trial every moment in time. We are God's witnesses. We are called to be His witnesses in word, thought, and deed—these three, in an order. First, by communication, in word; second, mentally, in thought; and lastly, in practicality, in deed.

Death is a normal event in life. Death is normal for those who have run the race and used up the allotted span. The Canaanites here, being human themselves, view this mourning in Jacob's family with a measure of empathetic understanding. They too must die. Their reaction to this mourning is to measure it. They say it's a "deep mourning." The most respectful and beneficial mourning is a mourning that actually touches your heart, faces the reality of the loss, and enables you to go deeper into yourself, providing a platform, firmer than before, from which to journey on lighter. Trying to stay light in the face of death is not deep; it's more likely to be denial.

And after he had buried his father, Joseph returned to Egypt, he and his brothers and all who went up with him to bury his father.

—Genesis 50:14

chapter fifty-five

THE CORRYVRECKAN WHIRLPOOL OF DOUBT

When Joseph's brothers saw that their father was dead, they said, "Perhaps Joseph will hate us, and may actually repay us for all the evil which we did to him." So they sent messengers to Joseph, saying, "Before your father died he commanded, saying, 'Thus you shall say to Joseph: "I beg you, please forgive the trespass of your brothers and their sin; for they did evil to you."' Now, please, forgive the trespass of the servants of the God of your father." And Joseph wept when they spoke to him. Then his brothers also went and fell down before his face, and they said, "Behold, we are your servants."

—Genesis 50:15–18

After all these years, all the evidence of Joseph's forgiveness, acceptance, love, and provision, and yet still his brothers still doubt! They're afraid that they will still be made to pay for their past sins. Is this not like the believer today who is diagnosed with a serious illness in later life and instantly recalls his sins as a cause for this illness?

The brothers sent messengers to Joseph! How quickly families can disintegrate when a father dies or leaves! Likewise, when a pastor leaves or a godly grandmother or mother dies. They are unseen ties, beautiful influences, and nets that secure us. Suddenly they are gone. Be aware in such times.

Joseph wept when the messengers spoke to him. Why? Because his brothers were still so estranged from him that they were afraid to speak directly to him. Hadn't he done enough to reassure them? Why didn't they believe him? Hadn't he demonstrated his love practically? Yet they couldn't speak to him. They actually thought he would respond with their own habitual weakness. *"Perhaps Joseph will hate us, and may actually repay us for all the evil which we did to him."*

How confused unbelief is. Unbelief feeds itself with the insecurity in the believer. The believer who doubts has just opened a whirlpool of sad despair. There's a whirlpool off the west coast of Scotland. It's among beautiful coastal waters normally easy to navigate, even in small vessels. At certain tides and times, the Corryvreckan whirlpool begins to turn on itself. It spins itself into an increasingly deeper place, and the careless and foolish are sucked into its cold, terrifying downward deathly spiral. Such is doubt. So is unbelief. It can remain dormant for periods, and you may never experience it, but given the right circumstances you can be caught, pulled in, and lost in a sea of despair. You must read the charts if you would sail in these beautiful waters. You must understand the tides; you must know the signs or never sail that sea!

So what are these spiritual "charts"? Where are these godly "signs"? What are the tides and times that set doubt on its whirlpool of despair? They are surprisingly simple; there are no super surprises. No need to study, no programs to follow, no counselling required to reverse it totally! The answer is in the simplest of Christian teaching and practice.

To fail in your Christian life and become a doubter, simply stop reading your Bible daily. But don't stop using your computer or keeping up with news and watching the media or following current trends in world opinion. These are tides that militate against spirituality, against faith, against trust. They are, in this day and age and for the last fifty years, totally anti-God. They are enemies of your soul. Yes, we should keep up to date with a certain level of world affairs and cultural trends, but never forget that they are just the newest in a series of ever-changing unexamined opinions. They will eventually be ditched unceremoniously and thrown in the garbage with all their devotees in favour of the next newest fashion in media and world opinion. The day is past when the church had an influence, so the world has gone after a great delusion, or many great delusions! So these are the tides.

The solutions, the safety nets, the "charts," are the same as they have been since earliest days. *"Have faith in God"* (Mark 11:22). Feed your faith by reading your Bible as often as you eat food; by daily, regular, and constant prayer; by diligent watching for opportunities to share your faith and the truth of the gospel every day; and by maintaining fellowship with godly people in a good church. By these you will never fail. No one who is diligent in these basic Christian practices will backslide. All who stop them backslide inwardly, outwardly, or both. Those who do their daily habitual reading without thought or heart or application and those who recite prayers like a heathen mantra will still die from spiritual malnutrition eventually.

Beware also of one of the greatest enemies of a real relationship with God, the church culture. That is the happy, friendly, social church that never does anything serious for God, that has all the external accoutrements of evangelical faith and even doctrine but is lost in its own inward interests and stuck in its culture of deadness.

Spiritual life is not evidenced by happiness or friendships or good food and great music. It's not at all evidenced by buildings or money or important people. The evidence is in the prayer life of the church and its deep, serious hunger after an understanding and application of the Scriptures to daily life. An increase in numbers is not an essential component. However, we should never be satisfied with no growth.

Doubt can be dormant, and you must constantly fight against it. If you don't militate against doubt, doubt will militate against you! There's no friendly, happy diversity program, no open system. Doubt is an enemy to be fought and defeated and kept under strict observation!

So are you a believer? Do you believe that Jesus has forgiven you and cleansed you of sin? Then never, never, give in to the suggestion that bad things that happen are God punishing you for past sins. He has forgotten them and moved on to greater interests in your life.

Joseph was sad, and he wept because of this trend in the brothers. They were his brothers, yet inwardly they had not dealt with doubt, and at this moment in the narrative, it assails them with fear and reduces them to lies and schemes, and all the while Joseph just loves them like God loves us, like God loves *you*!

chapter fifty-six

JOSEPH'S REASSURANCE TO HIS BROTHERS

Joseph said to them, "Do not be afraid, for am I in the place of God?"

—Genesis 50:19

Joseph's sees it as God's place to punish sins, God's place to judge and deal with His children. Joseph is saying, "I'm just your brother."

"*But as for you, you meant evil against me; but God meant it for good, in order to bring it about as it is this day, to save many people alive*" (Genesis 50:20). Joseph here sets the theological rule for Christians when we see evil and its results in our own life or in the world or in another's life. He says, "*You meant evil against me; but God meant it for good.*" What an amazing belief set is Christianity! Look no further for wisdom and grace for life. Your search is over when you find Jesus and walk with Him. No other philosophy, no other religion, comes close to the heights and depths of truth that Christianity reaches with such simple short sentences. Even a child can understand the words of Jesus.

"'*Now therefore, do not be afraid; I will provide for you and your little ones.' And he comforted them and spoke kindly to them*" (Genesis 50:21). See here a picture of the love of God in Joseph's assurance to his frightened brothers, "*Do not be afraid.*" See the women near the empty tomb when the risen Christ appears to them. Hear His beautiful words "*Do not be afraid*" (Matthew 28:10). How often in the Bible these words are spoken by God to His children! So, are you, dear reader, hearing them? "*Do not be afraid!*"

"I will provide for you and your little ones." What a gracious, thoughtful, real assurance, an assurance that went beyond the brothers to their children. Joseph *"comforted them and spoke kindly to them."* Words that speak comfort, like *"I will never leave you nor forsake you"* (Hebrews 13:5); *"I am with you always, even to the end of the age"* (Matthew 28:20); *"But the Helper, the Holy Spirit, whom the Father will send in My name, He will teach you all things"* (John 14:26); and *"I will come again and receive you to Myself"* (John 14:3). These words speak comfort.

But note a lesson for all of us: Joseph *"spoke kindly to them."* The Holy Scriptures take the trouble to tell us this because we desperately need to hear it! How hard it is to speak kindly in certain circumstances! Unkind words reduce the comforting words to less than nothing. They take the comforting words and use them to beat the weak into further misery. How we wish we could retract them, undo the damage, and repeat the comforting words without the unkind attitude or inflection. We may never have intended them to be unkind! Often kindness is in the form of an exhortation to a good thing—good faith, good trust, good encouragement. But unkindness is often just a whisper of an inflection, just a look in the eye, just a careless shrug, and it can be as poisonous to the needy as the brothers' hatred was to Joseph. Unkindness can be simply a disengaged heart behind the comforting words.

How did Joseph know that his brothers needed kindness as well as an assurance of food and physical care? He knew because one day he had needed kindness, and he didn't get it from them. But here he enacted a gospel standard set later by Jesus: *"Whatever you want men to do to you, do also to them"* (Matthew 7:12).

May God enable us to learn comforting words, especially spiritually comforting words, and to also learn how to speak them kindly.

chapter fifty-seven

DEATH OF JOSEPH

So Joseph dwelt in Egypt, he and his father's household. And Joseph lived one hundred and ten years. Joseph saw Ephraim's children to the third generation. The children of Machir, the son of Manasseh, were also brought up on Joseph's knees. And Joseph said to his brethren, "I am dying; but God will surely visit you, and bring you out of this land to the land of which He swore to Abraham, to Isaac, and to Jacob." Then Joseph took an oath from the children of Israel, saying, "God will surely visit you, and you shall carry up my bones from here." So Joseph died, being one hundred and ten years old; and they embalmed him, and he was put in a coffin in Egypt.

—Genesis 50:22–26

That is the life of Joseph. Like him we all will die and be buried in a good place in hope, surrounded by loving, believing family members who live in harmony. May God grant this to you, my dear reader, after a long and faithful life.

Thank you for reading this book. I pray that God will make it meaningful in your daily walk with Jesus, all the way to heaven.

ABOUT THE AUTHOR

I became a believer when I was thirteen. At seventeen, I felt a clear call to the Christian ministry. It came when I read this verse written by Paul: *"the hearts of the saints have been refreshed by you"* (Philemon 1:7). That notion of refreshing God's people by His Holy Word came to me as a clear call to the Christian ministry. That call and that passion have never left me to this day.

I had so many doubts and fears regarding the awesome responsibility and my own fitness that I didn't go into the ministry until I was forty-four. By that time I had worked for years in the engineering industry, the pharmaceutical industry, and business, where I learned about myself, life, and men as they are. I was concurrently a highly committed member of two wonderful Bible-believing churches. There I learned about the things of God and God's people as they are!

Eventually, and only after the persistent pressure of friends and the Holy Spirit and a further seven years of university, I was ordained a minister of the gospel in a Baptist church in Scotland, where I served for twelve years. I then received a call to a church in Ontario, Canada, where I served for thirteen years. My passion throughout life, and especially during my twenty-five years in pastoral ministry, has been to teach the Scriptures, to "let the Bible speak," and to share the gospel of Jesus Christ at every opportunity. At this point in life I hope to continue in that calling and perhaps, humbly, share the Word of God with a wider audience via writing.

When wee David, faced with Goliath, took up his sling, he said, *"Is there not a cause?"* (1 Samuel 17:29). As I take up my pen, dear reader, I say to you, Are there not still giants hurling insults at God's people? Are God's people not frequently abused, misrepresented, hated without cause, sold into slavery, and alone? Sadly, many members of the family of God have been made to feel solitary by their own brethren, just like Joseph was. Is there not a famine of the Word of God, and have we not become weak for want of it? Then find your Bible again and read it again.

Joseph was equally tried and tested, all by our loving heavenly Father. But by a solitary persistent faithfulness, Joseph prevailed. So may we, by the Word of God.

I have been married to Helen, a nurse, for forty-six years. We have four adult children and three grandchildren. I have many interests, including old cars, music (acoustic and bass guitar), archery, photography, and watercolour painting. I'm a Scotsman who left Scotland, the "Land of the Bible" (as it was known in better bygone days). I came to Canada, this land of milk and honey, in 2003 to serve a church as interim pastor for six months. God had different plans! The church called me to be their senior pastor, and I accepted. My family joined me in 2004, and we served the Lord there for thirteen years. In 2016 we received the priceless gift of citizenship in Canada. Somewhat ironically, to achieve Canadian citizenship we had to swear allegiance to the queen of England! God has a sense of humour and knows how to keep a Scotsman humble!

Also by the Author

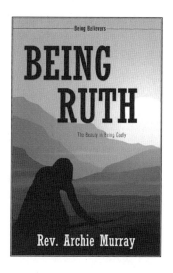

Being Ruth
ISBN: 978-1-4866-1709-8

Have you ever felt like your faith was being tested? Have you ever experienced the death of a loved one? The book of Ruth, found in the Old Testament, is a moving story of a sad tragedy followed by an unrelenting commitment, both human and divine. Ruth's sadness is followed by hope deferred, yet undeterred.

Being Ruth takes a closer pastoral perspective on the shape of human expressions and relationships, the significance of names, and the consequences of men dying childless. We see Ruth, the committed daughter-in-law to Naomi, responding with grace during a difficult time in life. Although this is not your typical love story, as you allow the Scriptures to speak you'll find a beautifully enchanting story.